I CAN'T BE DEAD

MARYANN OPAL

ISBN 978-0-9888387-0-3

Editor: Thomas N Opal
Proofreader: Michael T Opal
Cover Art: Matthew T Opal
Cover Design: Dawson Baker Graphics/Bethany Hand
Printed by Gorham Printing, Centralia, WA, USA

After reading this book, please write a review on Amazon.com

This book is dedicated to:

My brother Jay, who shouldn't still be standing, but he is. I love you Jay.

Tom, my husband and best friend;
Matt, my musician; Mike, my writer.

Each of you is so very integral with who I am today, how I arrived at this point in my life, how I have developed as wife and mom and, yes, student. You have taught me much, and I am indebted. You have helped me much, and I am thankful. You have loved me much, and I am blessed.

Thank you for all your help as I struggled to put my life on paper, for the creative cover design, for proofing my many-scripts and refraining from deleting some of my 'cheesy/campy' phrases. But most of all, thank you for your unwavering support as I wrote this book. I could not have done this without you.

I love you, Mike.
I love you, Matt.
I love you, Tom.

My memories may not be your memories.
My reality may not be your reality.
My truth may not be your truth.
This is my story.

Dear God,

It is so lonely in the house, I love coming outdoors. During the day, my favorite thing is to lie in the tall grass and look for you in the clouds. At night, you come to me in the stars. When I am outside, I feel you right next to me; sometimes I even feel you hugging me.

I love talking to you, and I try not to ask for too much. But I have been thinking all day, now that I am five years old and have started kindergarten, I hope you know I am old enough to know what I am talking about.

God, when I grow up I don't want to live like this; it just doesn't feel right. So I want to ask you a big favor, and I promise I will do my part and work really, really hard. I will not leave all the work up to you. There is a lot I could ask for, but there are really just three things that are most important to me.

God, when I am grown, can you please help me to have matching furniture, to marry a man who is not at all like my Dad, and to learn to speak properly?

Oh, and one more thing... sometimes people say "God told them." Please do not tell anyone this conversation because they will tell me to stop dreaming. Let's keep it our secret.

There is no greater agony than bearing an untold story inside you.

— MAYA ANGELOU —

ONE

The Appalachian Mountains are a study in contradictions. They are a land of beauty and peace. During the spring and summer, the brilliant greens of the hardwood forests glow in the sunlight, interspersed with the rich, darker green shades of the copses of coniferous growth. Sporadically, sunlight filters down through the branches, creating a scumble of shadows in varying hues of green. Dense growth covers the surface of the slopes that rise steeply from the surrounding grade, creating an impression of softness and serenity. Grasses in varying shades of green, yellow and brown sway in the mountain breezes as if worn by Hawaiian dancers, undulating first this way, then that, mesmerizing in their motion, ever different yet never changing. Butterflies flit to and fro in that maddeningly random pattern, that still manages to produce a sense of careful orchestration by some unseen conductor.

Autumn in the Appalachians is unmatched in its sheer grandeur and beauty. Each morning, the night skies slowly give way to gradually lightening gray, then to the pinks and oranges of the coming dawn until, at last, the sun scales the heights and sets the peaks ablaze with color. Shadows flee down the slopes before the onslaught of light and color until even the deepest valleys are a mural of autumn glory, a riotous display of fiery red, brilliant orange, and sunny yellow splashed across the endless slopes as if flung down by a gigantic paintbrush, still intermingled with the dark evergreen. In the late afternoon, darkness begins its slow creep up the very slopes down which it fled precipitously that very morning, gradually overtaking and extinguishing the blaze set by the morning sun. Finally, the highest peaks are the only color which can be clearly seen, standing high and proud, the last bastions against the encroaching darkness, beacons of light drawing the eyes on and ever onward to the furious display in the sky as the sunset turns the clouds into a living canvas. Eventually, the last rays of sunlight are chased into the west, replaced by a light show of a different kind as constellations in the clear night sky provide a new luminosity to the landscape.

Late in the year, beginning on the highest peaks, the mountains transform into the alien organic as winter softens the ridges with blankets of snow and the trees, which just a few weeks earlier sported brightly colored clothing, now stand almost nude, naked bark barely covered in scraps of white. Shallow streams and slow moving waters are coated in a layer of thin ice while at the base of waterfalls, rime glitters on branches and rocky paths, always dangerous, become impassable.

But looks can be oh, so deceiving! One only needs to peek just below the surface to understand that this is also a land of strength and hardness, for under the soft surface layer, whether foliage or snowdrifts, lies harsh bedrock and precipitous cliffs, stony soil and treacherous terrain, isolation and loneliness. It is a wild place, inhabited by all manner of wild beasts and cloaked in a mantle of even wilder growth—massive forests, meadows and swamps where tangled vines as thick as a man's arm defy passage of any but the smallest creatures, where brambles leave clothing and flesh alike in tatters, where poison ivy and poison oak run rampant, interspersed with stinging nettles and patches of saw grass.

It was this land that greeted the early pioneers of America as they began to push inland from the coastal regions in search of the new earth, better and richer. It was across these mountains that the settlers had to pass ridge after ridge of axle-breaking bedrock, slope

4

upon slope of threatening gravity, to be fought both up and down, thick virgin forests through which they had to clear trails and rivers they had to ford. Those who pushed through to the other side found those verdant lands and greener pastures. They found stable and level ground, and stood upright.

Others, for one reason or another, decided to remain in the mountains. The extreme terrain kept these settlers isolated from the world around them. Settlements developed more as enclaves than communities, with distinct dialects and a language structure audibly archaic and European. Though inhabitants invented musical instruments, many of the songs were handed down from the ancient ballads sung for centuries in their native lands. Cultural development in Appalachia was virtually devoid of contemporary outside influence, generation after generation raised without any real knowledge of the rest of the world. Government was of the people and by the people in its purest form, enforced with gunshot as deemed necessary. For nearly two and a half centuries, the Appalachian people remained invisible to popular America. Over time, these 'mountain people', named so as they were discovered, became a reflection of the surrounding ridges: strong and hardy with a backbone of bedrock, proud, beautiful, treacherous, wild, and free.

It is here my story begins.

My parents were from the Deep South, my mother from the birthplace of the Confederacy, South Carolina, and my father straight out of the Appalachian Mountains. Following World War II, they joined the mass migration from the South to Detroit, Michigan, chasing the promise of plentiful jobs and money in the automotive industry. Packing their belongings, they followed the old US-23 to Monroe County, Michigan, where they settled on flat ground. They were not, though, alone: US-23 was nicknamed 'Hillbilly Highway', a thoroughfare out of the Appalachians, from the mountains to the plains. Nestled safely among their most valuable possessions were the ways, culture and language of those mountains, transported directly to and set down in the Midwest. Adaptation to, or integration into this new culture never crossed my parents' minds. They thought nothing of setting up their own little Appalachian subculture in the heartland of America nearly a thousand miles from their home.

The force of my parents' will to inject their own history into the Midwest necessitated a house of extremes, not just emotionally but architecturally. Each of the four rooms in the house measured eight feet by twelve feet, for a grand total of 384 square feet of living space, and without a hallway to connect them, the layout felt like a maze, something to be navigated carefully and timed perfectly. My house missed also an indoor bathroom. For us, it was the outhouse most of the time, and during the night the only slightly better option of a chamberpot. Somehow, Daddy decided it was my brother Jay's job to empty it, and I tried not to use it unless I really had to, hoping to make things easier for Jay.

As a child, I had no concept of so many of the things that most Midwesterners take for granted when it comes to their houses. Windows, for example, were few; my bedroom had none at all, making it feel, alternately, like a safe haven or a prison, depending on what was happening on the other side of the door.

Our kitchen couldn't be called modern either, with just a small sink and two tiny ledges on either side. Our range, an old gas model, made me extremely nervous when we had to light it. I always felt that, with one wrong move, the whole house might explode. Was I so incorrect? In the center of the room stood an old aluminum table and folding chairs. The chairs didn't match, which bothered me. Kitchen sets were supposed to match.

The furniture in the living room didn't match either, the pieces all broken down. I thought that we'd probably be more comfortable sitting on the floor, except that sitting a little higher let me rise above the stench of the overflowing ashtrays set all around the room and made it easier to feel the heat from the potbelly stove, the one source of heat for the entire house. My room stood next to the living room but not nearly close enough to the heat. Winter nights, the glass of water I kept next to my bed formed a layer of ice on top. During the day, I tried to warm myself as much as I possibly could, thinking I might be able to hold onto the heat during the night; I still have a big scar on my left hand from inching closer and closer and then too close to the stove.

Although the cold was tough to endure, summers were really no better, since the windows and doors had to stay open so air could circulate. The screens were either full of holes or nonexistent, so flies always filled our hot little house. Other pests, like spiders and mice, inhabited our unfinished basement with a sand floor, aptly termed, a Michigan cellar. With no direct access to the house proper, the cellar also became home to sundry other pests, of the two-legged variety who were charged exorbitant rental fees for a dank, damp 'apartment'.

Everything about life seemed more difficult in our rustic little house. I remember feeling really excited when my Daddy got us a wringer washer. Until that time, we literally wore our clothes until they were as dirty as they could possibly get before throwing them away. The new washer sat outside, because that was the only place we had running water, and we hung everything on a clothesline to dry.

The washer was both a miracle of technology and a novelty, and I loved to use it. But even miraculous novelties must be handled with a certain amount of care, as I soon found. One day, as I was inserting laundry items into the wringer, I did not realize I was also feeding my long strings of blonde hair right along with the clothes. Clothes and hair, hair and clothes, the wringer continued pulling until my head was pinned against the rollers, the machine grinding with its efforts to

7

forcibly remove my tresses by their roots so it could finish its work for the day. Screaming in pain, and at the thought of having a huge bald spot on my head, I yelled for Daddy. He ran out of the house, moving as quickly as I have ever seen him move, and jerked the plug out of the dangling receptacle. Helping me untangle my hair from the rollers, he scolded me the entire time about my carelessness and stupidity. Needless to say, the washer didn't seem quite as exciting after that.

Our house, little in the big country, would have looked right at home sitting on any ridge in the middle of the Appalachian Mountains. Our family conversations, dialect and content, never went beyond the ridges of the mountains. Though there were no mountains for hundreds and hundreds of miles from our home, we lived in the midst of the Appalachians. With great pride, and with an accent only spoken by the Appalachian people, my parents repeated the cliché, "You can take me out of the mountains, but you can't take the mountains out of me." My parents had no knowledge or understanding of how living out that phrase would affect the lives of their children, forever. The path out of these mountains was treacherous, with many giants along the way, but was no less necessary for me than it was for my parents.

Out of suffering have emerged the strongest souls;
the most massive characters are seared with scars.

— KHALIL GIBRAN —

TWO

"Ken, you wouldn't hurt the baby now, would you?"

I remember hearing my mother speak these words as I sat on her lap, her embrace so tight that it hurt. Momma's body trembled as the smell came closer and closer, the smell that wafted between Daddy's bottle of moonshine and his lips. Her arms wrapped themselves tighter and tighter around me, and I started to shake along with her. My Momma always shook her foot, but that day I could not tell if it was her foot or my body doing all the shaking.

I stared at his eyes. They looked so different than when he was the storyteller Daddy, the one who kept us spellbound for hours and hours with tales about his home in the Appalachians, and the people who lived there, and all we wanted was for him to keep going forever. Those eyes sparkled blue. They could be soft and twinkly. They belonged to another time and place.

But not these eyes—I called them 'Crazy Eyes'. These eyes were dark with anger, unhappiness, paranoia and discontent. These eyes said he could hurt anyone. These were the eyes that caused us all to sleep with loaded pistols under our pillows, the same eyes that greeted visitors at the door with a loaded gun pointed at their chests. These were the drunken eyes that searched for threats in every look, every vocal inflection, every bodily inflection. These eyes bore witness of the tortured being inside, while the outer man waved his handgun around, letting off a shot every now and then just to remind friend and foe who was in control; literally, who was calling the shots.

Struggling to breathe, I opened my mouth, but nothing came out. I tried again, and squeaked out, "Daddy, please don't hurt us. Daddy, you love us. Why are you so mad? What can I do to make you feel better, Daddy?"

Almost as familiar to me as his Crazy Eyes was the single, dead, unblinking eye of the gun barrel. Although I had never gotten used to the sight, I no longer felt paralyzing fear when I looked into the eye of his gun. I knew it was loaded—it was always loaded—and it would do what it would do, according to my Daddy's whim. I learned to put my focus on him, not the weapon in his hand.

Wiggling free of my Mother's grasp, just enough to take a deep breath, I dug deep for a smile and tried to make my voice as loving and kind as it would let me. "Hey, Daddy," I said. "How about if we turn on the record player and dance to Loretta Lynn?"

He didn't budge.

My Momma's knees fidgeted beneath me.

"Daddy, please? You love Loretta Lynn, and I do too. Let's dance."

His face still glowed with something like hate.

With a gulp, I opened my mouth to sing, hoping the sound would be there when I needed it. *"Well, I was born a coal miner's daughter..."*

Ever so slightly, Daddy's eyes relaxed at the corners. The hard glint softened, and I knew he was picturing himself back there, in the coal mines, smelling the dust and feeling the dark.

"Daddy, tell me the part again about when the mine collapsed and your leg was trapped and you had to be rescued."

He closed his eyes and began to sway, nearly losing his balance. I took my cue and sang Loretta's next lines. *"Well, I was born a coal miner's daughter in a cabin on a hill in Butcher Holler. We were poor but we had love that's the one thing that daddy made sure of, he shoveled coal to make a poor man's dollar."* Slowly, I crawled down from my Momma's lap, took Daddy's hand and led us over to the record player.

As the real Loretta Lynn's voice took the lead, I sang along with her and held tight to my Daddy's hand. He turned me around and around, and I tried my best to help him balance so he didn't fall, relief like a compress for my fevered skin.

As soon as the dance began, I saw my Momma slip out of the room, away from her problems, back to her bed. As always, I made it better. I cleaned up the mess.

And as always, I watched Daddy's eyes for clues, for the quickest path back to safety. This time, when I saw them begin to fade into beautiful hues of blue, I knew he was back home, back to his happier days in the Appalachians.

In control, I led Daddy to the couch, singing all the way, and gradually helped him stretch out his body and drift away. Tip-toeing out of reach, I prayed that I'd handled enough for this day, and hoped for a better tomorrow.

But for my faith in God,
I should have been a raving maniac.

— MAHATMA GANDHI —

THREE

"Will the circle be unbroken, by and by, lord, by and by...there's a better home a waiting, in the sky, lord, in the sky," bellowed my Daddy in the most cow-like, yet angelic voice.

"MaryAnn, I believe. Do you believe?"

"Yes, Daddy, I believe."

"MaryAnn, I tell every person that walks in that door that I believe."

"Yes, Daddy. I know you do."

As he handed me the black fake-leather bound Holy Bible, he said, "Hurry along, the church bus will be here any minute, and we don't want Mrs. Cline to have to climb down those bus stairs to come looking for you. Some days, I don't even know how she makes it to church, nonetheless picking up all the neighborhood kids. Oh, and here, MaryAnn," he added. "Don't forget the offering." He handed me an old beer can with the top cut off and a piece of paper taped over the opening that had scratched upon it, 'The beer that made Milwaukee famous and made a damn fool of me'.

I measured its weight in my hand, happy that it felt so full this time. Each person who came to visit during the week was asked, and, if necessary, pressured to put money in the can. Daddy wasn't one to take no for an answer, and visitors knew they may as well put money in the can when they arrived, because they would be nagged until they did, and the visit would be much nicer if they got it out of the way sooner rather than later.

I grabbed the can and ran out to catch the church bus, hoping that, this week, I looked good enough for God and his friends. I slipped a hand up to touch my hair, knowing that the little tangles under the smooth outer layer of dirty blond had been there for weeks. I fought with those same snarls last Sunday. As I looked down at my clothes, I wondered if I had on the same outfit as last Sunday too. With only two good dresses to choose from, I lost track of the pattern sometimes. Determined not to care, to think about the true meaning of church, I sat myself down on the bus and tried to look forward to the soul scrubbing I was about to receive.

Once we got there, I walked sheepishly into the church, knowing my dress didn't really matter one whit, since most heads turned the opposite way as I walked past. There were some saints in that church, people I would call true saints, and it was because of those folks that I went back week after week. During those weeks, which turned into months and then into years, I came to realize that God could and would carry me through anything. With all my heart, I believed him when he gently whispered to me, *"When you pass through the waters, I will be with you and through the rivers, they will not overwhelm you. When you walk through the fire, you will not be burned or scorched, nor will the flame kindle upon you."* (Isaiah 43:2)

A short old woman with blue-gray hair picked two boys from children's church to collect the offering each week. To me, it looked like the same two each week, but maybe it wasn't. Maybe they just looked the same to my searching eyes; tall, dark, and handsome in their neatly-pressed suits. One stood at each end of the row, as the round wooden offering plate, lined with red velvet peeled upward at the edges, passed my way. Without shame, I dumped my offering out of the beer can and into the hands of God. The miniature ushers always grinned from ear to ear. I always grinned back at them, until the week I saw that their eyes didn't really mean to be kind, but I never stopped giving the beer-can-money. Because Daddy believed, I believed.

Children's church was always the same. The highlight was Bible Quizzing: each week, the same little old lady called out a scripture, and the first one to find it and read it aloud got a point. By the time I found the word she pronounced in the index, one little usher had already jumped up and started reading. I never did get to read one of those verses, but I would have if those boys didn't have perfect attendance. Some weeks, as I glanced down at my worn out Bible with yellowed pages, I wondered if it would be wrong to pray for those boys to be sick just one Sunday. Just one.

I loved going to church, the one time of the week when the dark clouds of fear and loneliness gave way to bright sunshine. Most kids seemed glad church was over, celebrating as they ran up to their moms and dads and jumped into their arms. Instead, I hurried back to the church bus to ride into the unknown, a little sad to be finished because I knew a Sunday afternoon could go any way at all, no matter how light my heart or strong my faith.

The dragging of the bus tires on the gravel road caused me to look up as we approached my house. When we stopped, I saw my Momma waiting at the end of the driveway, a sight rarely seen. I swallowed hard and tried to make up some reason that it was a good thing but nothing came to me.

The eyes of the bus driver always shone with pity, and this sunny day was no exception. How could one look so sad and worried on such a beautiful day? As I hopped off the bus, I noticed my Momma's eyes were sad too, and the left one was swollen. They glittered with fear. Because people's lips rarely spoke the same words as their eyes, I learned to listen to their eyes and, on this day, my Momma's eyes clearly signaled her fear, and a warning.

Covered with trees, bushes, tall weeds and broken down buildings, the field across the road was perfect for playing hide and seek, and perfect for hiding from my drunken Dad. When I got off the bus, my Momma pulled me so hard that my hand ached as I tried to keep up with her.

"Your Dad has been drinking moonshine since you left this morning. The more he drinks the more he rambles about all his kids leaving him, and now you're gone too."

The other kids had all found an escape route, each using a different method to get out, to run as far as they could, glancing back only because of their love for Momma and Daddy, two of the greatest people in the world, except when they weren't.

And as alcohol mixed with my Daddy's already confused mind, it got harder and harder for him to remember simple things, like the fact that if I was gone to church, it did not mean that I was gone forever.

We hurried farther and farther into the field, and the high, untended bristles scraped my arms and legs with each lurch deeper into the weeds. When my church craft and my treat fell to the ground, I wanted to stop and search or at least protest over my loss, but I didn't say a word because I knew it wouldn't matter.

I didn't have to ask Momma if Daddy hit her, but I did have to ask why. "Did he hit you because he was sad about the kids leaving?" I said.

"Honey, there is no way to know what goes through a drunk's mind. That's why you can never trust what your Daddy is going to do next. It's not predictable and it certainly is not logical."

Once Momma felt we were far enough off the road, we stopped for a much-needed rest. Her pitiful eyes glanced at the scratches covering my body, then quickly darted the other way. "Sssh, do you hear that?"

My heart beat out an unsteady rhythm.

A car drove very slowly past the field, and my Daddy's slurred voice called out, "Mae, I'll kill you, I'll kill you."

We had heard this many times before; it seemed killing some-one was always on my Daddy's mind, so the words didn't scare me as much as they should have. We continued to hear the car creeping up and down the road, as well as my Daddy's voice, though most of the words were indistinct. Then came the sound that I had learned to fear, a gunshot. All the blood in my body plunged to my feet. I nearly toppled over.

Daddy was rarely seen without his pistol; it seemed most often as he was shaking it in someone's face, eyes bulging as he shouted obscenities or growled threats through clenched teeth.

Now, tires on gravel, gunshots and my Daddy's slurred words... our obvious clues to keep running. By way of the field, we ran into the backyard of our closest neighbor.

"Can you keep MaryAnn here? Ken is on the warpath again, and I have to see if I can get him calmed down and in bed."

"No Momma, please don't go. He might kill you. Please Momma, don't go."

As she walked out of the front door and into the road, the neighbor told me to hide in the dryer. I hesitated, not sure if I could make myself climb into such a small space. My head throbbed, fear poking at me from all directions. With a deep breath, I climbed inside the cold, hard metal compartment and prayed I wouldn't have to stay long.

The claustrophobic feel, combined with the darkness of the dryer, scared me even more than the repetitive, familiar fear of my Daddy and the gunshots. What seemed like hours later, I heard a car pull in the drive, a knock on the door and my Momma's voice. She opened the dryer door, grabbed my hand and said, "Come on, let's go home."

We walked in the house to see my Daddy, passed out in his bed, pistol on the headboard. Nothing more was ever mentioned about the day. Just another Sunday afternoon—what was there to talk about?

That which does not kill us makes us stronger.

— FRIEDRICH NIETZSCHE —

FOUR

Though my Mom invited people in need to use our garage apartment, my Dad saw that space in far more concrete terms and, more often than not, sought out his own sort of strays to bring in extra money. And, while the folks my Mom collected tended to be harmless, I never knew what might happen with the garage 'friends' my Dad found, for whose lodging the only requirement was cash in hand. One such friend, an old man nicknamed Peg, because of a war injury requiring the amputation of his leg, taught me more than I ever wanted to know about secrets.

The first secret of Peg's home actually belonged to my Dad. When he decided to rent out the garage, my ingenious Dad made the place look more appealing by building walls out of two-by-fours covered with cardboard. He then wallpapered over the cardboard, floor to ceiling, to give the impression of solid walls and no one but the unlucky few who leaned in the wrong place ever knew the difference. My Dad was resourceful, creative, and could pretty much make anything from nothing. I wish those walls had been the only thing about the garage that wasn't what it seemed.

At first, I thought Peg was a nice old man. He would tell me how lonely he was and ask me to come and visit. He told me war stories, and I listened intently. Even better, he promised me candy. Candy! In my house, there was no money for something like candy when the nonessentials were so hard to come by. How could I resist such an invitation?

Of course, when I got there, I found out that the candy came with a price tag, something that made me feel sad and uncomfortable and helpless, something that Peg liked to call 'our little secret'. And though he told me how much he loved me and how special I was, before long, I started to hate the sight and smell of this man called Peg, this waste of skin, just as my stomach started to hate the sight and smell of candy. He was the monster not in my closet or under the bed, but in my garage.

When I'd had enough, I decided I didn't need to feel helpless anymore. Waiting until the sun went down, I hurried outside to the garage, hands full of the corn kernels we fed to the chickens. Feeling powerful, I ran in circles around the building, throwing handfuls of feed at the windows. In a drunken stupor, Peg stumbled from window to window on his one good leg, trying to see who would dare to pick on a 'lonely old man'. I dashed back to my house, extremely pleased with myself. It was a small effort, but at least I was fighting back.

What I didn't know was that Peg had caught a glimpse of me out one of his windows, and told Dad what a bad little girl I had been. When my Dad heard what I had done to his friend, a man who claimed to adore me, Dad gave me the one and only spanking of my whole life.

Devastated, I learned a lesson that I carried for years; telling was against the rules.

Man performs and engenders so much more than he can or should have to bear. That's how he finds that he can bear anything.

— WILLIAM FAULKNER —

FIVE

As soon as my eyes opened, I looked at the newspapers covering the floor, newspapers with a big red X on them, which meant danger. Without even pausing for my body to stretch, my mind started working. Did Dad come home last night? Which warpath would he be on?

I sighed, thinking for the millionth time that Saturday mornings on television were never like this. Folks had time to lounge in their jammies, to relax for a moment before the worries of the day set in. Certainly, they had time to stretch. My hands crept up to rub my temples. If this were a weekend morning on a TV sitcom, the show might even be a bit humorous, but it wasn't and it was not; this was real life.

Every Saturday morning, it was my brother Jay's chore to mop the linoleum floors, after which he was to cover the freshly mopped floors with newspaper while they dried. Jay devised the system of using red crayon X's to warn the rest of us as we awoke. If the path led outside through the front door, it meant Dad was home, because a path leading out the back door would have taken us directly past his bedroom.

Being as quiet as possible while walking on the newspapers, I followed the red path. It took forever to get to the front door, though our house was small. With each step, I stopped and held my breath, striving to hear my Dad's snoring over the deafening sound of my heart. I hoped to feel the presence of one of my sisters, Rose or Sue, coming in to take my hand. Rose, having filled the role of 'Mommy' almost more than my mother, offered the protective maternal instinct. Diametrically opposite, Sue was a fighter, the one who would never give in and say 'monkey's uncle', the one who would fight off Dad as long as possible. The journey outside felt so much shorter and so much safer when my hand was clasped tightly with one of my fellow warriors.

Swinging open the front door, the morning sun greeted me and the fresh air bid me good morning. For a second, I didn't have a care in the world. Nature wrapped her arms around me and all was well.

The door banged shut behind me, and I jumped, immediately flushed with guilt. My sisters scurried to my side. "Shhhhh. We told you so many times not to let the door slam shut. You'll wake up Dad."

"He came home just when the sun came up, sat at the table and had a couple of whisks of moonshine, before Mom begged him off to bed."

"When we came out he was still awake, but, hopefully, by now he is sound asleep."

Together, we ran through the tall grass to our favorite tree, huge with lots of winding branches, which made it extra fun to climb. My siblings and I had rigged it into a tree house of sorts, pieced together from all kinds of stuff from the dump. I giggled when I saw it, the trail of the red X's nearly forgotten.

Just big enough for the three of us, we occasionally squeezed a little tighter and made room for Jay if he wanted to join us. We didn't have to worry because he would only stay long enough to say, "This is really cool," and then he would find his way back down to the ground. A shelter through many storms, the tree offered us a great deal of comfort. In fact, I often wondered, as I watched my brother climb out and away, why he didn't stay a little longer and bask in its safety.

The very best thing about the tree was that Dad was afraid to climb it, although he wasn't afraid to fire a shot that caused the leaves to fall at our feet.

I settled back into my sisters' warmth and listened to the soft rush of wind in the tree branches. This was what Saturday mornings were meant to be like. I wished the feeling could last forever. I wished every

Saturday could be like this. Happiness washed over me from head to toe.

A blood-curdling scream split the morning air. My insides twisted and I remembered the red X's on the newspapers and why we were in the tree house in the first place. There was just nothing to be done when Dad got on one of his mean streaks, something that always seemed to happen when he came down off a binge but would not sleep. Terrified, we hurried out of the tree and followed the cry until we reached our brother. I gasped and cried, wanting to help but only feeling immensely powerless.

I stared at Jay, shirtless and dressed only in jeans, hanging by his belt loop on a long railroad spike pounded into the wall. His skinny body looked pitiful, vulnerable, and totally helpless. His big beautiful crystal blue eyes showed only fear. What else could exist in that moment? His gaze begged us to do something, knowing that if he had any chance at all, it was that Dad wouldn't want his little girls to see him behave as this horrible beast. We three girls formed a circle around Dad, wailing, screaming, crying, and begging him to leave Jay alone. I looked up at my brother, broken and defeated. My heart ripped right in two.

My Dad always carried a large, sharp knife in his pocket, and he used it often, both to aid his creativity and as a weapon. I didn't know how he intended to use it that day, and, by the look on my brother's face, neither did he. Slowly pulling the knife out of his pocket, Dad emotionlessly flicked open the wicked blade and reached toward my brother. Time stood still. As one, we girls held our breath while Dad, with a small smile and a barely audible 'snick' as fibers parted, cut the belt loop, leaving Jay in a heap on the ground. And as one, we now hugged and kissed and squealed with excitement as if Dad had just won the world whittling championship. Quietly, but thankfully nonetheless, we went into the house and picked up the newspapers from the floor. The danger was over for now.

As for Jay, he just looked over his shoulder to glance at us before quickly disappearing into the woods. The wild expression on his face provided a clear glimpse into his future. No one is equipped to survive such insanity.

A piece of Jay died that day, a big piece.

Those who dance are considered insane by
those who cannot hear the music.

— GEORGE CARLIN —

SIX

The chickens twirled around and around, as if to the music of a rock band playing in their heads. Their heads, however, were lying about fifteen feet away, clustered on top of our garbage pile. And right in the middle of the flock, twirling in time to the unheard beat, I spun and pirouetted like a dervish, feet tapping out the spastic rhythm of the chickens, arms flailing wildly, hair flying in all directions as I capered madly back and forth. Momma and Daddy laughed until they snorted at the sight of me dancing with a bunch of headless chickens. Hungry for the sound of their amusement, and thrilled to be the center of attention, I danced until the last chicken dropped.

"You are something else, MaryAnn," Daddy said. "Lucky you still have your head, dancin' around with them birds."

"That's 'cause I dance better than them, Daddy," I giggled.

That fall I entered kindergarten, and one day my gym teacher said we were going to do the Chicken Dance. I immediately launched into the routine I'd done for my parents, shoes squeaking on the polished floor as I mimicked the spinning, stumbling chicken bodies. I waited for the appreciative laughter and, when none came, I stopped and stared back at the children staring at me.

My excitement slipped away as if a bucket of cold water had been emptied over my head, drenching my very being and awakening me to the fact that most of the people I encountered that first year of school thought very differently than I did, almost as if we came from different worlds. As I progressed through the grades, I learned those worlds were even more different than they seemed that first day in gym class.

Of course, at home, nothing ever changed or even gave me hope that change was possible. And when harvest time rolled around, just like clockwork, we followed the same steps every year, starting with boiling and plucking the headless chickens.

Two of our biggest pots sat on top of our gas range in preparation, the water in them boiling so hard it splashed over the top of the pan. Daddy carefully brought the buckets to the back stoop and, one at a time, we dipped the chickens in the water to scald the feathers loose. The smell of the chicken sinking into the boiling water always made me gag, and I wished I could run to the chicken coop because the smell of fresh poop would have been such an improvement.

We then plucked out the feathers one by one, laboriously picking even the small tufts of down. After the last feather was plucked, we placed the chickens on the wooden step, and with our biggest butcher knife, chopped off their tough, taloned feet. A good rinse and the chickens were ready to be cut into fryer parts and frozen until the next time Momma made fried chicken, or my favorite, chicken and dumplings. Because we froze most of the meat for the long winter months ahead, we kept the gizzards in a separate pile and fried them up for a treat at the end of our long day. By the time we got to eat them, I sure felt like I'd earned those gizzards.

"Stop eating so many, MaryAnn," complained Sue. "You're not special, just 'cause you're the baby."

"Hush, Sue," my Daddy barked. "Let her eat what she wants."

I smirked at my sister and grabbed another gizzard, happy at that moment to be right there with my family, crazy as we were, working together to take care of us all.

Fall brought thoughts of winter, and with those thoughts came the realization that we had just a short time left to can, freeze and preserve our food. All the small game that Jay had hunted over the summer, things Momma always found a way to cook, was almost gone, making room for the new harvest. We'd eaten many legs from the frogs Jay speared, and though we tacitly agreed to say, "Jay's gone rabbit hunting again," to describe the times he escaped the house and sought shelter in the woods, he did often use that time to trap rabbits, raccoons, fish, squirrels and anything else he thought we might be able to eat. Momma never knew what she might have to dress for supper once Jay returned from 'rabbit hunting'. But the summer days full of fresh food were coming to an end, and we needed to prepare for winter.

Whenever Daddy slaughtered a pig, he insisted on boiling its head to make head cheese, or, if pickled, souse meat. So, once again, we put the biggest pot on the stove, until the water roiled into steam from the boiling pig head. The stench was overwhelming; we had to go outside and throw up, only to come back in and keep cooking. After boiling the pig's head for hours and hours, came the tedious job of picking all the meat off the bone and skinning the tongue.

Wait a minute, got to go spill my tummy...

Once all the meat was picked off, Daddy, who had a hand for flavoring headcheese, mixed in about as much spice as we had meat. Ever so delicately, he ladled off the gel of the broth and poured that over the meat, then put it in the refrigerator to let it set. Perfectly spiced and perfectly jelled, Daddy's headcheese brought people out of the woodwork, mouths watering and compliments flowing as he beamed with pride. Once the smell had dissipated, I have to admit, I did like a bite or two of souse meat. My favorite part of the pig, though, were cracklins. Nobody cooked cracklins like my Momma.

But my favorite memories of harvest time are the fresh garden vegetables. Grocery stores have never seen produce the likes of what came from our humble garden. Oh, how I loved the canning operation, it engaged all my senses, filling me with pleasure. Day after day, as the pots roared to a boil, canning jars stood scattered about on dish towels, waiting to receive their gift from the garden which they would later bestow upon us as the harsh Michigan winter caused supermarket prices to skyrocket. Day after day, I was greeted with the aroma of fresh boiling tomatoes, the squeaky feel of corn husks as I shucked the cobs and the sound of green beans snapping. Night after night, after a dinner featuring the most delicious array of flavors, my eyes drank in the splashes of color spread across every available square inch of kitchen, spilling over into the other rooms.

One by one, my siblings disappeared from the kitchen as I sat there, wide-eyed, for the entire process. Momma knew potatoes were my favorite and she would pop bits of potato into my mouth as she worked, smirking each time she handed me a piece straight off the paring knife. Beans, peas, bell and banana peppers, cucumbers; I wanted to taste it all. It was then that I understood why she worked in the garden day after day, year after year until sweat rolled down her face.

But above all, I loved seeing my Momma so happy and so proud of her accomplishments.

The hunger for love is much more difficult
to remove than the hunger for bread.

— MOTHER TERESA —

SEVEN

"Please stop, Daddy. Please!"

I ran out of the house, my feet set in motion as soon as the goat's wails floated through the open windows. "Not Henrietta!" I screamed. "Please don't hurt her!" I tore across the yard at full speed then stopped, just as fast, at the sight of my sweet little goat, tied so that she could only move a few inches, side to side.

My stomach lurched, waves of nausea pushing higher and higher with each pitiful cry. In each tortured bleat, I heard it all: the pain, the surprise, the sadness. Henny and I talked all the time, whenever I hid myself with the animals to escape whatever might find me inside our dreary walls. We spoke each other's language and, just as Henny listened to me share the horrors inside my home, the things no one else wanted to hear, now I heard the sound of her horror, and the hurt nearly broke me wide open.

"Help me, MaryAnn. Help me," she moaned.

Frantic, I stared at my Daddy, at the bloody sledgehammer rising and falling in time with Henrietta's pain. "Daddy, please, please, please..."

"Go on inside, MaryAnn. You shouldn't be out here."

"You shouldn't be doing this," I screamed, desperate to move closer and do something to help, but my feet wouldn't move.

"Help me, MaryAnn," Henny cried again, as blood poured from her head.

I gasped and lurched forward, as if I could grab either the sledge-hammer or Henny's broken body and remove it from Daddy's reach.

"I told you to get away, MaryAnn," he said. "I have a job to do. A family to feed."

I covered my face with my hands, suddenly knowing what I had not allowed myself to know, that the animals were just food to Daddy, meant to be eaten, no exceptions. No matter how much time I spent with them, no matter how much their gentle presence saved and distracted me from the wrath of my house, when Daddy decided it was time to eat, that was it.

I took one more look at him, at the sweat dripping down his face and the strange, eerie peace in his expression as he pounded the sledgehammer faster and faster into Henny's head.

I never knew what to expect from my Daddy; he was a walking oxymoron, complete with two legal identities; names, birth certificates, social security numbers, and driver's licenses. I lived with the fear of calling him by the wrong name in a given situation. Legally and emotionally, my Daddy could change his identity in the blink of an eye, and he did. I guess this is why he was so successful as a loan shark and a drug dealer, a man whose clients never knew where they stood with him, or for that matter, which him they stood with... and neither did I.

Even so, I couldn't move away, I couldn't let my friend make her last sounds without someone who cared nearby.

When the noise quieted, my body took off, back across the yard and into the house that had never before seemed like a safe place. That day, however, I couldn't bear to be outside, couldn't stand the thought of being in the animals' world, of seeing their beauty and then seeing it crushed. I ran to my room and put my head under the covers, but the sound of Henny's cries stayed in my head no matter how deep I burrowed. The agony haunted me, that night and for years of nights to come.

No change of circumstances
can repair a defect of character.

━━ RALPH WALDO EMERSON ━━

EIGHT

"Hurry, Dad. I see the bus."

Dad rolled his eyes like he did every morning as I called for him to walk me to the end of the driveway. "Ten years old and I still have to walk you to the bus. What a shame."

My stomach clenched. The real shame was that my father, my protector, allowed a vicious animal to roam free in our yard, terrorizing me every morning and every afternoon with its fierce determination to rule our little plot of land. The thought of walking our driveway alone paralyzed me. I needed my Dad to stand between me and the beast or school simply would not happen.

Dad and I headed out the backdoor and down the stairs. As we hit the bottom step, the creature met us there. Large and confident, he made me gasp and hold my breath. Beautiful does not even begin to describe him. Glossy, speckled underbelly highlighted proud copper plumage; his sharp, hooked beak was indeed a regal nose. The crown that sat with stately aplomb upon his head was of pure, fiery, burnished garnet. There was no doubt about it; Rex ruled our yard.

But as with all things Appalachian, exterior beauty was only a cover for underlying strength and hardness. Sinewy legs, battle-scarred and muscular, gave the impression of enormous power, yet moved with the grace of a ballerina. Mighty talons adorned his feet, talons meant for rending and tearing, for leaving foes ripped and bleeding, their life force pouring from deep gashes only to be eagerly lapped up by parched soil always thirsting for its next bloody drink. The plumage on his wings was the color of dried blood, yet glossy as if that blood were freshly spilled. The vivid red comb stood like a spiky mohawk, the only part of his body that did not absorb all light in the immediate vicinity. Rex was one scary rooster.

He and my Dad stared each other down. Rex puffed his feathers and flocked toward me a couple of times. My Dad, wanting to prove who was boss as much as he wanted to protect me, took one giant step forward and commanded the rooster to leave me alone. Rex tossed his head and inched to the side, staying about two feet from me as we walked to the bus. Every few steps, he jumped toward me, forcing my Dad to call him off time and again.

Pulse racing, I fixed my gaze on the door of the bus and tried to see nothing else. I nearly pranced, trying to be light and quick, to cover as much ground as my skinny legs allowed. Rex clucked and complained at my heels and mine alone, never once striking out at my Dad.

As I got on the bus, I felt only seconds of relief before I started to worry if my Dad would remember to come back to meet me when the bus dropped me off after school. All day long, whether I was learning math or running in gym class or watching a filmstrip in science, Rex sat in the back of my mind. Beautiful despite his evil nature, he loomed larger than life in my imagination. At day's end, perched on the first seat in the row, nose pressed against the window, I longed for the sight of my Dad at the end of our driveway.

When the bus stopped at the end of our driveway, a huge stick lay twisted across the rocks at my feet as I exited the bus, my Dad's way of telling me he would not be meeting me. Panic flooded my throat. I had to fight the rooster myself.

Trembling, I picked up the stick, which stood taller than I, and turned toward the drive. As soon as I crossed the gravel road, Rex saw me and immediately headed my way. I said a little prayer. How could I possibly have posed a threat? I had never done anything other than run from him. I took a deep breath and tried to catch his eye, to see something new in his gaze.

He glared back at me, the same Rex as always. He was a fighter and he fought for blood. His main goal in life was to prove himself, and he used his huge, thick spurs to achieve that goal. Just plain mean, the kind of mean that caused most people to fear him, he reinforced that fear with his speed and the height at which he flogged.

The monster didn't move, not attacking, neither retreating. He stared into my eyes and I shuddered. I'd seen those crazy eyes before. I would have to run and hide or I would have to fight; there was no middle ground. My heart raced. Slowly, I took another step. He didn't move. Another step; still no movement, just a baleful stare. On my third step, he lurched forward and I gave a little yelp.

I tightened my grip on the stick. *You can do this, MaryAnn.*

"Out of my way, Rex," I squeaked, trying to imitate my Dad's commanding tone from that morning.

Rex's sharp features scowled. He danced about me, gleefully slashing with his talons, leaping into the air and beating his powerful wings, all the while screeching out the most hideous sounds ever to be given voice. My mouth dried and I glanced across the yard to my house. I might as well have been walking to Chicago.

Body stinging, as if every bit of exposed flesh prickled and bled, I tried to swing the heavy stick, as the sound of my salvation tore up the gravel. Too focused on the rooster, I hadn't even noticed the approaching vehicle, but my eyes misted with relief as I recognized the distinct sound of our car. Skidding into the driveway among a shower of small stones, the driver got out with a mighty slam of the door. I smiled up at my Dad as best I could. The man I may have found myself hiding from the night before, the other brawler who fought for blood, grabbed the stick from my hand and shook it right in Rex's face.

"Mess with my baby and I'll kill you," Dad growled.

Ken, I went out the other day to look for eggs and the rooster got me bad. I could not find nothing to hit him with so he beat my legs up bad. I could not kick him off, the more I kicked the harder he flogged me. He hurt my foot. I had a big knot on it. I could not walk all day. I was going to kill him but I decided not to. I am going to put him in the wire cage that's in the yard. That rooster is real bad, when you are not here he gets after everybody. Love, Mae

Original letter my Mom wrote to my Dad while he was away visiting family in the Appalachians

Faith is taking the first step even when you don't see the whole staircase.

—— MARTIN LUTHER KING, JR. ——

NINE

Day after day, I listened for the watermelon truck, for the sound of the gears shifting like no other vehicle that traveled our gravel road. As soon as I heard it, my lips tingled with the need to smile, and I danced along the driveway, waiting for the words stenciled on his door, 'Jasper Jones', to appear before my eyes as the truck made its wide, slow turn into my path.

No matter what the truck called him, however, I knew the driver as 'Jap', and the list of things he taught me was both long and life-changing. Most of all, I learned that, in the midst of the chaos that defined my life, small things could make a big difference and, with hard work and faith, dreams really did find a way to come true.

Even when I was a small child, my Mom and Dad stayed in bed all day. They were there, but they were not there, a horrible way to live. In a very real way, Jap became my voice in an otherwise silent world. When I heard him coming down the road, my insides leaped with joy and, as soon as he appeared, I ran to him and jumped up into his truck.

As soon as I climbed in the cab, he hugged and squeezed me as if it had been years since he greeted me this way yesterday. "It's been so long since I've seen you, girl. What in the world have you been doing?"

That question, of course, was my invitation to tell him every one of my stories, even the ones I had told him the day before. I talked and I talked, and the dear man listened and smiled and laughed, always saying, "Girl, you are quite a storyteller," which made me feel like there could be no greater calling in life.

And in the rare moments when something left me speechless, Jap taught me the power of the puzzling phrase. Time and again, in times of awkward silence, I watched him smile, shake his head, and toss out some colorful comment that got everyone to thinking. "Funny fishes, them mack'rel," he'd say, or, "Long time between gateposts." My favorite was, "Kiss my grandmammie's axe handle," which never failed to make me laugh out loud.

Jap always had a way of making me feel better about how things were when he wasn't around. When Dad had beaten Mom until her face was contorted or when he had been drinking, Jap would tell me, "Sometimes your Dad has a hard time making good decisions, but he's sleeping now. Let's look for a rainbow."

With his gentle wisdom, Jap set a new standard in my troubled life, teaching me the true meaning of colorblindness and pureness of motive. He taught me that it's easy to whine, but it takes a very big little girl to keep smiling when she doesn't see anything to smile about.

Best of all, he would tell me, "Your Mom said I can be your god-father, so you are lucky. You have two Daddies."

One of the very best gifts this 'second daddy' ever gave me was the power to decide early on that I had to move forward in the direction of my dreams, no matter what others thought. Dreaming and working for the dream always came hand in hand for me. It never occurred to me to make a wish and just sit around and wait for it to happen. So when Jap talked about the freedom of owning his own business, my mind took off like lightning.

Though very few cars drove down our country road, I decided there had to be a way to capitalize on those that did pass by the end of our drive. After a lot of thought, I set up the most beautiful produce stand I could manage, complete with signs that begged everyone to 'Stop Here'. Filled with big, bright red tomatoes, potatoes, green beans that actually snapped, corn, cucumbers and any other produce I could dig from the garden, my stand featured better quality and a larger variety of produce than the local grocery store, a reflection of the great pride my Mom took in our patch of vegetables. My grin grew wider at those cars that passed but quickly slowed and then stopped. Who could refuse a little girl with a big dream?

Alongside my vegetable display, I placed a big piece of cardboard decorated with a picture of a horse, drawn using every color from my sixteen-count box of Crayola crayons. Between the fresh vegetables that caused everyone's mouth to water and the vivid picture that captured the imagination, my little roadside stand quickly became a hit. And with each sale of beautiful produce, I told my customers of my plan to buy a pony, my voice full of excitement and belief.

Looking at me then, I'm sure the landscape, with our waist-high grass, ramshackle house and decrepit outhouse, did little to make believers out of those who passed by. Clearly, we had nowhere for a pony to seek shelter in inclement weather and obviously not enough money for food to keep the poor creature standing. The logistics hadn't crossed my mind yet, but, for me, having the dream was just a matter of figuring out how to make it happen.

Each day, late in the afternoon, I would hear that watermelon truck coming down the road, definitely a highlight after sitting in the hot sun hour after hour. As soon as he turned the corner, I would see the big smile on Jap's face and feel my face light up in response.

"How was business today?" was the usual question, as he climbed down from his truck.

"Kinda slow," I invariably responded, "but there's a little more in my pony jar."

With an approving nod, he would remind me that sometimes entrepreneurship was like that, then he would launch into a business discussion—some of which I understood, most of which I did not, but all of which I liked to hear—speaking to me as he would another adult. "Well, girl, some days are good and some are not, they call it the ebb and flow. The key is to keep going, never quit."

Every day after our talk, Jap would say, "Let me see what you have left. I could use some fresh vegetables, especially ones that look this good." He would then buy all the items left on my stand, which, though it took me a long time to get them all set out beautifully, actually amounted to only two or three of each variety. Patiently, Jap waited while I laboriously added up the cost of all the vegetables and then he paid me the exact amount, even if it sent me scrambling for the correct change. Jubilant, and naively thankful that I had been able to sell all my vegetables for the day, I would then clean everything up and jump into his big truck for the drive up to our house.

"I sold all the vegetables today," I would yell into my Mom and Dad's bedroom when we stepped into the house. They usually congratulated me, often woke up long enough to smoke a cigarette, then rolled over and went back to sleep.

On his way into the living room, Jap would set his vegetables on top of the refrigerator. Day after day, I told him he might not want to set them there because he forgot them the day before.

"Lordy mercy, girl," he said. "I did, didn't I?" Sitting down in the same chair as always, he would pull his cigar out of his pocket and started rolling it around in his mouth, never once lighting it, though the charred end looked like he must have done so at least once.

When the huge cigar came out, giving off the scent of burnt vanilla, I would sigh in delight—this was my cue that I could begin telling him my stories again. I loved this time with Jap. He was so kind, sincere and funny, always making me giggle. The time flew by, and all too soon it was time for him to leave. On his way out, he always stopped by my parents' bedroom, who, before depression, alcohol and drugs took over their lives, loved these visits with Jap as much as I did, to bid them farewell. They sat up and chatted with him long enough for another cigarette, then off to sleep they would go, and out the door he would go, my world instantly turning lonely once again.

Without fail, as I turned to go back into the living room, I spotted his vegetables on top of the refrigerator. Like a shot, I ran out the back door and called out after him.

"Aw, girl," he would say. "I'm too tired to come back in tonight. Why don't you see if you can sell them tomorrow?"

So the next day, I would put them back on the stand, add some fresh vegetables, and the story would play out much as it had the day before, and the day before that, and the day before that...

After many such tomorrows, one day Jap asked me if I was close to my goal. With no idea how much a pony cost, I assured him my money jar was getting fuller by the day. He told me he knew someone selling a pony and suggested we ask Mom and Dad if we could go look at it.

My parents instantly said no, reminding me that we didn't have anywhere to keep a pony and certainly no way to feed it. My heart sank almost to my feet. I pleaded and promised that I would figure all of that out.

"Let us know when you do," was their answer and that was that. Trying to control the sobs, I turned from their room and ran to hide in mine. Never missing a beat, Jap stopped me and said we had better start working on a plan before someone else bought the pony. Bolstered by how much he believed in me, my tears stopped and my hope rose anew.

Jap and I drove down to the farm where Rose and her husband Butch made their home, and I told them I thought I had enough money saved to buy a pony. Explaining that Mom and Dad would not let me get one, I asked if they could help me think of a plan, if somehow one of their many barns could help me realize my dream.

After lots of talk, Butch smiled at me. "You can keep your pony in one of the stalls in the barn if you promise to come down and take care of it every day," he said.

I squealed in delight. "I promise," I said and came up with the idea of getting off the bus at their house and taking care of my pony before walking home.

Butch, having been born and raised on the farm, knew the food grew right in his own backyard. "You help us with our crop," he added, "and we will give you food for the pony. She'll need some added grain, but if you work hard enough we will buy that with your earned wages."

My chest swelled with joy. Holy cow. Did we really just solve this humongous issue in one sitting? Along with Jap, Rose and Butch, the God of the Universe must believe in me too, I decided.

Jap and I jumped in the truck to go back and tell my parents the plan. As soon as they heard that Jap and Rose and Butch were involved, there was no further discussion. Those were three people that they trusted. No need for them to listen to the details; that might take energy.

That night, I fell into bed happier than I'd been in ages. The next day, Jap and I were going to look at the pony. I couldn't sleep a single wink.

The next afternoon, when I heard the beautiful music of that watermelon truck's engine, I ran inside to get my jar of money. By the time Jap pulled into the driveway, I stood ready and waiting.

"Girl, you got battery acid on your feet?" he said with a grin, as I pranced from foot to foot, impatiently.

I smiled back and told him that must be the case because my Dad always asked me the same question. I started to jump into the cab, but Jap held up a hand to halt me and slowly opened his truck door. I ran to his side, desperate to be on our way but fighting to be patient.

Jap didn't do anything fast, but, that day, he seemed to move in extra slow motion. He climbed down to the ground, "I have to check the watermelons before we go, 'cause I heard some moving around back there," he said.

We walked to the back of the truck, he opened the gate, and I gasped. There stood the most beautiful pony I had ever seen. Our eyes and our hearts connected. I reached out to touch the silkiest coat I'd ever felt on any animal, a glossy shade of brown like homemade apple butter. My pony. My dream. Mine.

Unable to stand still, I hugged and squeezed and thanked Jap. Together, we took my dear pony down the road to her new home, and I talked nonstop about how no pony would ever be more loved or better cared for. When we finally headed back to my house and he came inside as always, I proudly handed him the jar of money, which he promptly forgot on top of the refrigerator when he left that evening.

In this bright future,
you can't forget your past.

— BOB MARLEY —

TEN

"Let's see what the rich folks left us today," Dad said as he started the car.

On Saturday morning, no one had to be told to get out of bed or hurry up and get ready. Our favorite time of the week, this day we got to go digging for treasures. If we waited long enough, pretty much anything we needed eventually showed up at the dump. I learned to have patience, keep high hopes, and be willing to dig to the bottom of several piles, most of which were twice my height, until my long-awaited treasure revealed itself. Sometimes, it took a month or two, but eventually we found everything on our list.

Even better than finding an item from our list, however, was the unexpected discovery. As the triumphant pronouncement echoed up from another part of the dump, "Look what I found!" everyone ran over to check out the newest treasure. If you found it, it was yours—that was the golden rule—and we each took turns having great success and, even if we didn't find anything for ourselves, had a great time oohing and ahhing about what the others found. One weekend, I uncovered a watering can with some plastic flowers glued to one side. I gave it to Mom and she was so happy about it that I began turning over all of the plywood boards I found, hoping for yet another success. Although we used a strict finders-keepers code in the dump, violating that rule to give Mom a gift she liked so much pleased me more than just a little.

Our own version of family time, the dump was our favorite outing, and we giggled and squealed together for hours. At home, I didn't get to spend much time with Jay, but he loved going to the dump, and I loved that time with him. By far the best at finding treasures, he did not leave one thing unturned. In many ways, our trips to the dump brought out the best in our family, both our love and our creativity.

For example, having a telephone never crossed our minds, until Dad found one at the dump. He picked it up, gave it a twice over and said, "What do you think, MaryAnn? Do you think we can get it to work?"

Mom interrupted and said, "Ken, you can't just pick up a telephone in the dump and think you can make it work."

I looked up at my Daddy, our eyes connected, and he knew I believed he could do it.

Not only did we find treasures in the dump, we earned real money. We all came prepared with magnets and learned at a very early age how to spot aluminum. When climbing through the piles, we'd pull those magnets out of our pockets and test our knowledge. If the magnet stuck, we had a winner. Once identified, Dad helped us keep our aluminum separate from one another because, when he took it to the 'aluminum man' the following week, he wanted to be sure we each received the correct reward for our efforts. When a can from Mom's heap tumbled into the valley between ours, I considered toeing it into my pile while whistling into the air, but the air was too thick for whistling. Besides, I needed my hands to whistle and I was certainly not going to put them in my mouth there.

During the summer, the atmosphere became noxious as foul odors permeated the air, hovering around our faces, stifling our breath, making us gag. On those weeks, Sue didn't make any money as she pouted in the hot car, arms crossed and sweating. She would turn and look at me, then look back at the threads of the headrest and plug her nose with both hands, elbows cocked at shoulder height. One of those weeks, when she refused to come looking, I found a treasure that I will never forget: a bicycle, a real bicycle.

Buried beneath mounds of garbage, the handlebar caught my eye first, still wrapped on the end with ragged, but sparkly, plastic. I hurried toward it, knowing instantly that something great lay at the bottom of the pile. Determined, I moved as much as I could around the bike's frame until the other handlebar was revealed, planted my feet and tugged with all my might. I was waist high in waste. With one giant, creaking whoosh, the bike pulled free and sent a wave of trash mixed with sharp metal rushing toward me. Hanging on to those handlebars like I might drown, my feet slid out from beneath me and sent me tumbling into a sea of hard corners and sharp edges. Hurt and exhilarated, I screamed at the first injury the bike caused me.

Everyone came running—Dad because he knew I had found a treasure, Mom because she knew I was in pain. As they skidded to halt next to me, Dad patted me proudly on the shoulder and reached for the bike, while Mom stared at the blood gushing out of my knee.

"Ken I think we are going to need to take her to get this stitched up," she said.

Dad looked closer and gasped. Dropping the bike, he picked me up in his arms and headed to the car.

I wailed, louder and louder as we ran away, "My bike, my bike."

In a flash, Jay ran back, grabbed my bike and stowed it in the car for me before we headed to the hospital. Once there, the doctor asked what happened. As fast as an exited little girl could talk, I started telling him about finding my new bike. Dad cleared his throat and said, "You mean *riding* your bike."

I opened my mouth to tell him, "Silly Daddy, I don't even know how to ride a bike yet," but when I saw him giving me 'the eye', I pressed my lips to a close and blinked up at the doctor. For the first time, I realized the dump was another one of those things that we didn't talk about. No matter how excited I felt or how great the treasure I found, the dump was something to be ashamed of. My stomach churned with confusion. I sure didn't know why it mattered, but that was definitely the look I got from Dad. I swallowed and added the dump to my 'list'. Numbly, I answered the rest of the doctor's questions as my own swirled endlessly, unanswered.

The doc stitched me up and, after bending my sewn knee to test the new stitches, sent us on our way. Back in the car with my new treasure, I quickly forgot my pain and my confusion. The only thing I cared about was getting home to ride my new bike.

To this day, when I look at the scar on my knee, I get a warm fuzzy feeling.

To succeed in life, you need two things:
ignorance and confidence.

— MARK TWAIN —

ELEVEN

"Dad, this doesn't look so hard when the other kids do it," I said over and over again. "Am I stupid, Dad, that I can't learn to ride a bike?"

With the patience saved for me alone—no one else in my family got anything close—my Dad righted my dented bicycle and pulled me up off the ground. "Here, let's go try again, honey," he sighed.

Feet on the pedal, hands on the handlebars, I was once again ready to go. I narrowed my eyes and concentrated with every muscle.

Dad held on to the bike and ran along on one side. After a short distance, he let go and shouted, "Go, honey, go. You can do it."

I pedaled as hard and fast as I could, yet before I knew it, I was back in the same heap on the gravel road. Gritting my teeth, determined to feel the wind in my hair as I tore up the open road, I picked small bits of gravel from yet another abrasion, got back on my bike and tried again. Night after night, despite scraped knees and wounded pride, I kept trying.

"Dad, you have to run faster," I instructed. "I see the kids going really fast. Run as fast as you can, Dad."

He grabbed the handlebars and the back of the seat and ran as fast as he could until he was out of breath, then let go and, once again encouraged, "Go, MaryAnn, go. You can do it."

And, as always, the bicycle came to a spinning stop with me sprawled out; under, on top of and alongside my bike all at the same time. Dad grabbed me and the bike and ran to the house.

Sobbing, I said, "I'll never learn, will I, Dad?"

Hearing the commotion, Mom came running out, berating Dad, "Ken, what have you done now? I told you that bicycle was a piece of junk." She cleaned the badly cut knee and swabbed it with iodine, a staple in our house.

Before it was even completely cleaned, my knee began to swell, fast and big. In an instant, Patient Daddy disappeared and Mean Dad stepped in. "MaryAnn," he said, "when something swells that fast and that big, it's always cancer."

I gasped and pulled my legs up to my chest.

Chuckling, Dad went on and on, telling me about the pain to come and assuring me that I would probably die from this.

"Ken, leave the child alone," Momma pleaded. "You're gonna scare her to death."

Dad ignored her and continued to talk, convincing me that I had only a short time to live. Once again, Dad's character had changed on the spot; he was so nice, until he wasn't.

The next day, Rose and Butch stopped by. As soon as Butch saw me, he gaped at my knee. "Who did you get in a fight with?"

Frustration and fear bursting out all in a rush, I told him about trying to learn to ride the bicycle and I kept falling off but I really wanted to learn and it shouldn't be so hard to ride but now Mom was going to make me stop because the bike is just a piece of junk and I would probably kill myself before I ever learned to ride that is if the cancer in my knee didn't get me first.

Finally pausing to take a breath, I saw Butch shaking his head as he told me not to fret and went inside to reason with Mom. I pretended not to listen and hid my grin when Mom said maybe Butch could teach me, because he already knew how to ride a bike. How could my Dad possibly teach me, she said, when he didn't even know how to ride a bike himself?

Butch said, "Come on, let's go show that bicycle who's the boss."

As I proudly hopped on the bike, I instructed Butch. "Now, you hold on here and here, then run as fast as you can. I'll pedal and, when you can't go anymore, you let go and I'll keep pedaling." I looked him in the eye. "So far, I've fallen every time, that's why Mom doesn't want me to keep trying."

Butch shrugged and grabbed the handlebars and the seat. He started to walk.

"You have to go a lot faster than that," I told him.

Dad, who stood nearby acting like he couldn't care less, said, "She's right, you gotta run."

As Butch started to run alongside the bike, he glanced down and immediately stopped running as laughter threatened to make him lose his grip on my treasure, "Are you really trying to ride a bike without a chain?"

Dad and I both give him a puzzled look.

"Huh?"

Still smiling broadly, but with sincere kindness, Butch explained, "This bike is missing a chain, and no one can ride a bike without a chain. Honey-child, you're not the problem here, it's all in the bike."

With the utmost confidence he went on to say, "As soon as we get a chain on here you'll be off and riding in no time."

Those words sounded like they had come directly from heaven. My insides smiled as I understood that it was the bike that failed, not me. All my feelings of frustration gave way to even more determination.

"I will ride this bike."

And I did.

Everybody is a genius. But if you judge a fish by its ability to climb a tree, it will live its whole life believing that it is stupid.

— ALBERT EINSTEIN —

TWELVE

There he was, twenty feet in the air, dangling from two belts rigged into a harness, looking for all the world like some island tribesman scaling a palm tree. Hanging there, I was frightened that he might fall.

I yelled up to him, "Hey, Daddy, whatcha doin' up there?"

"Honey, I was thinking about one of them telephones like the rich folks have."

He stopped his work and looked down at me.

"You look like one of them workin' men with all them tools on your belt."

He did. He had several tools suspended from his homemade harness. They looked like any or all of them might fall off at any second.

"I *am* a workin' man, honey," Daddy corrected.

"No, you ain't, Daddy, you don't have a job."

"I'm workin' on this here phone, now ain't I?" he said proudly, no trace of bitterness in the words.

That stopped me and I didn't say anything for a second.

"Hey, Daddy, you remember that time I was tryin' and tryin' to get my bike up that big hill? I had to go get all stitched up, but I got it up there."

"Yeah, I remember, honey."

"Well, you and me Daddy, we know how to make stuff work."

He was holding a dirty phone in one hand. It might have been ivory at one time, but it had been worn to a tan. A corner was chipped off, leaving a black hole. It didn't look broken to me, though. It looked like many of the treasures Daddy found at the dump. It was scraped, scratched, old, and dirty, but not broken. There were several stains on the outside, as if a man had ignored the pleas of his wife to wash his hands and made a call after working on the farm equipment.

Daddy looked up at the sky. It was dull gray and blue. Clouds covered the sun. They hung, stagnant. I never liked cloudy days. A pall seemed to accompany clouds, like they carried spirits in them, and they covered the world when the time came.

"If these rains here hold off long enough, I think I'll be able to talk to the operator."

"Why do you want to talk to the operator, Daddy?"

"Honey, if you tell the operator who you want to talk to, she'll dial them up for you. Long as they have a telephone."

"Do you think Uncle Tobe has a phone in the Appalachians?"

"Lordy, no, honey. Them phones are only for northern folk. Now go get your mother and tell her we're gonna have a telephone."

I rushed up the driveway to find Momma. I was eager; anticipation tickled my legs and made me run faster.

Momma was in the garden, where she always was during the summer months, before depression and drugs. Tiny green shoots stood upright in neat rows, seeking the now hidden sunlight. Momma was near the end of one row, tending to the delicate vegetables. If everything worked out, she would grow enough food to feed us for the winter.

"Momma, Momma, hurry, Daddy's got a telephone and he's at the tip-top of the telephone pole and he's gonna dial the operator!"

Momma started at this. "What in the world would your Dad want a telephone for?" She looked up to the top of the pole where Daddy had his feet planted against the pole, leaning back against his makeshift trouser belt harness. He was grinning from ear to ear, the smile so big we could see it from the house. Momma jumped up and ran towards the pole, yelling the whole way for Dad to get down from there. Daddy's smile never faltered.

Reaching the pole, Momma demanded, "Ken, you get down from there. Right now."

Daddy slowly descended the pole. "I followed the wires from Timbers' phone to the pole and copied it as close as I can. I think I can get the operator."

Shaking her head, palm on her sweating brow, Momma griped, "Why are you always trying to make something out of nothing, Kenneth?"

I felt a spider in my stomach. I prepared.

Only now did Daddy's smile falter a little. Looking at Momma he mumbled, "Cuz I like to."

Daddy looked down at the phone and fiddled for a little bit with the phone, and then fiddled a little more. I saw Momma beginning to get impatient with him. Daddy fiddled a little more.

"Here goes," he said. He held the receiver up to his ear. Then he began speaking to someone on the other end of the line.

I looked up at Momma, my eyes wide and bright, filled with delight and pride at the resourcefulness of my Daddy.

"See Momma, Daddy *can* make it work."

Just keep taking chances and having fun.

— GARTH BROOKS —

THIRTEEN

The sun so bright, the snow so white; for as far as I could see, every-thing glowed white—the trees, the shrubs, everything. So beautiful, it looked like God shook a little of heaven down to earth, and I couldn't help but smile at the gift.

In a flurry of noise and movement, Daddy burst into the kitchen with boots and coat, or what he called his coat, though Momma wouldn't have let any of us kids wear such a thin jacket in the cold. "C'mon, kids. I know a way we can have some fun," he said, smiling like he himself had invented winter.

Momma sighed, the way she always did, and pressed her lips to-gether in that way that meant Daddy might be up to something. "Ken, what are you getting ready to do?"

As if he didn't hear her, he thumped around on the dingy linoleum and clapped like he didn't already have our attention. "Come on, kids, while I still have my boots on."

I peered at Sue and Jay, uncertain, as always, if it was safe to follow Daddy's lead. They glanced among themselves, shrugging and nod-ding, until the twinkle in Daddy's eye got the better of them. We eagerly but hesitantly threw on our coats and gloves and ran out the door.

Momma's voice echoed behind us like the howling wind, "Now you be careful with them kids, Ken."

"What are we gonna do, Daddy?" I asked, because he always seemed to like questions from me, even though my brother and sisters got in trouble if they asked questions.

"We're going sleddin'," he replied, and strode toward the driveway.

I couldn't believe my ears. I had wanted to try sledding for so long. God was shaking down some heaven for sure! "Where'd you get a sled, Daddy? I've seen the kids playing on sleds. It looks so fun." I danced along behind him and waved to urge my siblings closer. "Hurry! Daddy got us a sled!"

He stopped next to his old beater car and smacked her on the hood. "Here, let's get this hooked up and see if it works." He rattled an old, rusty chain and hooked it under the bumper, then stood back and grinned. I took a deep breath and tried to smile back.

"There, I think that'll hold," he grunted, tugging on the chain.

"Where's the sled, Daddy?" I bobbed my head high and low, anxious to get just a glimpse of one of the plastic tomato-red sleds all the kids at school described.

"Right there." He pointed at an old rusted hood from the truck that stood out back, the one he'd been working on until the weather turned brutal. Flipping the hood over, he hooked the other end of the chain on a metal ring at its edge. "Hop on, kids," he called and jumped into his car.

During the winter, Daddy started his car first thing every morning. More often than not, it would not start right away, forcing him to spend most of the morning trying to figure out what the problem was and the rest of the morning fixing it. He could not relax until he got the thing running. His fear, phobia really, of not having an operational vehicle in an emergency, was something I did not understand until he told us the story of his birth, which made me cry every time I heard it and made him dark and distant every time he told it. As the story goes, his mother went into labor and his father couldn't get to the bottom of the mountain in time to get to the doctor, so she died giving birth, dead before Daddy had even made it all the way into the world. For the rest of his life, Daddy carried the burden of 'killing his mother'. So starting that car mattered to him, almost more than anything else in his life. In fact, it sometimes seemed like only thing Daddy felt he could control was having that car ready to go in case of emergency.

I bit my lip and waited, hoping that today the car would not start, yet curious about how it would feel to sled Daddy's way. But the beater flared to life like a champ and, before he got out of the car and screamed at us all for not listening, Sue, Jay and I all jumped onto the car hood and held each other for dear life.

Snow rooster-tailed up from his tires like it exploded from a cannon and, in a blaze of exhaust and taillights, we flew down the driveway toward the road. I squealed in terror and delight, though the winter wind stole my breath and my voice as soon as they left my lips. I stared at my siblings, desperate to store the memory of us all laughing and holding each other. In the distance, we saw Momma's small frame dash down the driveway behind us, screeching threats at my Daddy and prayers for our safety.

"You bring them back here right this instant, Kenneth," she wailed. "Dear God, make that crazy man bring my children back in one piece."

I watched her swing side to side in the distance, then realized we were the ones bouncing and fishtailing down the road. I giggled and wished she would calm down. For once, we were having fun. Sure, the scent on Daddy's breath and the sled on the car probably didn't go together, but the chance to have fun only came when he smelled like that, and I'd learned to enjoy whatever I got, even if I only had seconds to do so.

Christmas... is not an external event at all,

but a piece of one's home

that one carries in one's heart.

FREYA STARK

FOURTEEN

"Wake up, wake up."

A massive hand, gentle but insistent, shook my shoulder. "Dad, please let me sleep just a little longer," I mumbled.

"Up you go. You know what today is and how much we gotta do before Christmas Eve." He gave me another shake.

I groaned and rolled over. "It won't be Christmas for weeks."

"Right, we only have weeks. Get goin'."

"Your stupid rooster hasn't even crowed yet," I grumbled. "At least let me sleep until he wakes up. Anyway, who wrote the law that we have to start preparing for Christmas the morning after Thanksgiving, and before the sun comes up?"

"MaryAnn, you know how difficult this time of year is for your Mom."

Curiosity sparked in my mind. I sat up and looked him in the eye. "Dad, why did she give away those babies?"

He frowned and pointed a threatening finger in my direction. "Don't you dare talk about that."

"You brought it up."

"I was just remindin' you that you and I have to work extra hard cuz this time of year takes her down. Now please get up."

Year after year, we had this very same conversation the day after Thanksgiving, and the very same silence about the babies. And, year after year, I sighed and got out of bed before even Rex knew the sun was on its way.

To begin, we scrubbed the house from floor to ceiling, including inside anything that opened, like closets and cupboards, which usually took a solid week of continuous work, every waking minute. By the end of that first week, our tiny house stood spotless, completely purged of the clutter that piled up from January to November. It even smelled fresh, and that was my favorite part.

After the scouring, we took the next week to paint every wall. This one time a year, I gave thanks for a very small house. Once the walls shone fresh and bright, we took a trip to Bargain City and bought four rolls of linoleum, at $13.99 each, to cover the floors. Despite being the youngest, I got to choose the paint color and the linoleum pattern. Dad both believed in me and relied on me to decorate, and I experienced great pleasure taking charge of this task. Because Christmas was one of only two days a year I could count on feeling joyful and loved, my young eye tended toward happy colors and patterns, designs that might let me hold on to a little bit of the holiday spirit when the darkness came back and eclipsed my memories.

The third week was spent decorating. I was allowed to choose all the decorations and place them as I pleased. Of course, my 'choices' were limited to what I could find at the dump, leftovers from neighbors and relatives, and items remaining from previous years. In this season of life, as I learned to use what I had and make my world beautiful, my creativity was allowed to flow. Our little house was sparkling clean, freshly designed and decorated for Christmas. It looked like a mansion, and Dad and I were so proud of what we accomplished.

Our work finished, we dedicated the final week leading up to Christmas to not getting one single thing dirty or out of place and, quite literally, counting down to the 8 p.m. Christmas Eve Party. With each hour, my excitement grew, snowballing toward the big event. My very favorite time of year, Christmas was truly a magical time in our home, with everyone on his or her best behavior—a fairytale family.

Each evening, we plugged in the Christmas tree and sat in the glow of love.

Dad would say, "MaryAnn, how long until the party?"

Always prepared, I would answer to the day, hour and minute.

With Christmas came presents, and with presents came shopping. In that week of waiting before the party, we set aside one day and everyone loaded in the car to head for Bargain City. I tingled with excitement as Dad handed each of us a ten-dollar bill to buy presents for our parents, our siblings, one special teacher and one special friend. My hand never touched such a huge amount of money at any other time of year.

Instructed to make it last, we knew well what that meant. When we pulled into the parking lot, Mom reminded us to put our coats over our buggies so our siblings could not see their gift if they happened to walk past. She also taught us that we might need to change the price tag if we wanted to buy an item out of our price range. "Don't let the store people see you doing this, but it really is okay. This is a huge store and it won't hurt the rich, northern folks to stop being so selfish and join in the Christmas spirit."

Following her directions to the letter, I always came home with the perfect gift for everyone, grateful that the kind folks at Bargain City had not made a fuss over the prices I selected. And when the party finally started, our tree overflowed with presents—the perfect presents for a fairytale holiday—exactly what each of us, including my parents, stressed over and searched for.

Christmas Eve at last, Mom and Dad appeared promptly, all dressed up and looking the best they had all year, with the perfect clothes, the perfect hair, clean fingernails, and cologne—a treat saved only for this magical evening. Mom even put on lipstick, even though she always said it made her look like 'a whore in church'. I thought it made her smirk just a little more mischievous.

At 8 p.m. sharp, my Dad stood and started the tradition that had been in place for all my Christmases. He picked up one present at a time, read the nametag, "To so and so, from so and so," and handed it to the appropriate person. The recipient then ripped off the wrapping and squealed with excitement; once again, Mom, Dad and siblings had selected the perfect presents. Hugs and smiles and gratitude filled the room.

Once they had distributed all the presents, Dad and Mom went into their bedroom and called us in one by one. Time for our stockings. We each received a brown paper lunch bag filled with nuts in the shell, an orange and a whole lot of chocolate. Squeals, a standard noise on Christmas Eve, filled our house, as if we didn't know exactly what would be in the bag. It didn't matter; as always, it was the perfect stocking. Mom and Dad beamed with pride at being able to, once again, grant us the best Christmas ever!

One year, as the special events unfolded, something seemed out of place, something I couldn't quite put my finger on. It seemed everyone else was having a 'bigger' Christmas than I was. I knew that my parents always spent the exact amount on each of us, literally to the penny. Thus, it made no sense to me why I should be feeling odd. I tried not to let it spoil the moment and danced around as usual, if a tad out of step.

In the midst of the festivities, the door rattled with a loud knock, and everyone looked up, surprised. Dad answered it, finding a big wrapped box, which he brought in and settled in the middle of the kitchen floor. Puzzled, I glanced around the room and saw everyone else felt the same.

Mom stepped over to join Dad at the box and then, in his official Christmas Eve nametag-reading-voice, Dad announced, "To Mary-Ann, From Santa."

My heart skipped at least twelve beats as I walked up to the box;

there had never been a gift delivered from Santa in our house. Feeling lightheaded, I opened the box and saw two of the most beautiful ebony eyes looking up at me: a puppy, a real live puppy. The squeals that were emitted from my mouth superseded any Christmas Eve squeals that had ever been squealed before. My legs danced like they meant it this time. This, THIS was the best Christmas ever! I reached into the box and picked up a tiny, chocolate ball of fur and energy, a poodle, a dream come true.

From that day forward, Coco became my best friend and my confidante. There for me during the lonely days and the fearful nights, he was an angel in fur.

Christmas, when the magic of heaven came to our house.

A letter from one of "those babies"

From the time I was very young, the same questions filled my head and my heart over and over again: Why don't I look like my sister? Why doesn't my sister like the same things I like? Of course, we were five years apart and, for a long time, I let the age difference be my answer.

In second grade, my mom and dad gave me my first clue about where I came from, a step I later learned they took because they worried that other kids in my class, after overhearing their parents talking, would start asking me questions. That day, they told me that I had been adopted, directly from the hospital, when I was only two days old. When I heard this, I felt it was true, since my sister always talked about being an only child and only getting one day of notice that a new sister was coming into the house.

Content to have some sort of an answer, I put the issue aside, and my adoption wasn't really discussed much until I was an adult, when my husband-to-be talked to my parents one night and started asking questions of his own. Tim had a right to ask, since I'd told him that both of my parents died in a car accident.

When my husband asked, my mom and dad told him that I'd come from a family with two existing children and that they did not have the means to care for a third. Hearing this after all these years of convincing myself that only death could keep my real parents from loving me and raising me themselves, I realized that there are other reasons for adoption than death. Once again, however, I pushed those feelings away and closed the door on the subject until a miraculous event on February 11, 1979 brought everything to the surface again.

On that day, I gave birth to our first daughter, the very first blood relative I had ever known. What a joy that was! I kept the joy of that connection to myself, though, and did not speak of it to anyone. I didn't want to hurt my parents by suggesting that their love somehow meant less because we had no biological connection.

With so many new feelings stirring, it occurred to me how many people are affected, in so many different ways, by just one adoption—easily twenty to thirty people per case. At that point, those questions from early childhood returned again and I started to be curious about who my blood relatives were, what they were like, where they lived, and if I looked at all like them. In 1994, I began looking for my birth family, to the point of asking myself if every person I came across looked or acted like me.

As I searched, I was given the phone number of the doctor who oversaw my delivery and, when I placed the call, the nurse I spoke to offered to provide the phone number of someone she felt could help me. Lo and behold, through a series of very quick events, only hours passed until the phone rang that evening. The biggest surprise of all was to hear what sounded like my own voice on the other end of the line, as three sisters all tried to get a few words in. 'When do we get to meet you?' was the first question out of their mouths.

From my perspective, I think adoption has a greater effect on the family giving up the child than the family that God blesses with a new addition. In this situation, my sisters knew they were missing a sibling who did not come home from the hospital. I, however, didn't start to learn what I didn't know until this very phone call.

And then, soon after, when we all made the five-hour drive to meet in person, there seemed to be an instant connection. For me, it felt as though, at 36 years of age, I found people who looked like me, acted like me, and like I had known forever. Suddenly, magically, I had more sisters, and it was so hard to believe how many things we had in common though we grew up in such different circumstances.

One of the most important things I learned, as I got to know my biological sisters, was how much I needed to thank God for removing me from what they grew up with, for sparing me the hardships they had to endure. I immediately saw this as more proof of God's hand at work in my life. He knew that I would not have handled that life as well as they did, and he protected me.

For my sisters, I give thanks that they were given one another to turn to in times of need so that they didn't have to go it alone—they had God and they had each other. Of course, this created a very tight triangle for them, one that I did not feel certain had any room in it for me. So, even after the wonderful experience of meeting in person, the questions did not go away. Would we continue on from there, becoming true sisters and friends, or would we just content ourselves with having met each other? I just didn't know.

Though my adoptive parents were blessed with the gift of a baby girl, and I was blessed to be raised by very loving and caring parents, I now saw firsthand the effects of adoption, especially after I learned that one more sister had been adopted out of the family. We were all working to put the pieces together, but there were far more pieces than any of us anticipated.

As for that other sister, given up for adoption three years after me, questions still remain about whether she will ever feel like she would like to meet the rest of us. If so, the door will always be open on my part, though I now see how complicated these relationships are. To this day, my sisters and I try to figure out who we are to one another.

As time passes, I understand more and more how important these decisions are. With my baby sister MaryAnn turning 50 this year, it's clear that none of us is getting any younger. We need to make time now, or we may not have time later. And while it still trips up my brain to think that I can be the baby of the family while also having a sister younger than me, I pray that none of these things will matter in the end and we will all find our way to one another eventually.

—Kathy Azzam

If you don't like the road you're traveling

on, start paving another one.

— DOLLY PARTON —

FIFTEEN

Laid out on the table: one loaf of Wonder Bread, one pound of sliced bologna, a jar of mustard, and one five-pound coffee can fully cleaned out. We had already stuffed the car full of pillows and blankets. Once Daddy started the car, he would not turn it off until it rolled into Uncle Tobe's driveway in the Appalachian Mountains. The coffee can was both a warning and a symbol of the interminability of the drive.

Daddy's longing for moonshine and his insatiable desire to return to the hills took our family to the Appalachians every spring and summer vacation. These trips will be etched into my memory for all time. They always began the same—taking our old beater car, usually purchased at a junk yard, to the local garage to get it in the best possible condition, hopefully running well enough to make the trip through the hills, although we usually ended up spending at least a small part of our vacation at a shade tree mechanic along the way. Our cars were single use, for this trip only, and by the time we got back home the engine was shot for one reason or another.

Special care, a disproportionate amount of care, was always given to the brakes because of the many hairpin turns we encountered on the narrow dirt roads in the Appalachians. The roads through the mountains had turns that seemed to fold sharply back upon themselves before mysteriously sending us off in a different direction. Knife-edge cliffs closed off half of our field of vision around these corners, and headlights on the road indicated a car only too late. So our brakes always had to be in the best condition possible.

Backing out of our driveway, Loretta Lynn blasting on the eight track player, Daddy and I would be singing at the top of our lungs: *"Well, I was born a coal miner's daughter..."*

Invariably, hiding a smile, Momma would say, "MaryAnn, if you are singing in parts, you can leave my part out."

Laughing, Daddy and I would continue to belt out 'Coal Miner's Daughter'. It's highly doubtful that Loretta Lynn herself would recognize our peculiar rendition, sung off-key, but with great enthusiasm. Our singing would continue unabated well into Ohio. Finally, the initial excitement of being on the road waned and, faced with the prospect of many more hours without a break, I faded in and out of sleep.

At Momma's insistence, Daddy would always wake me as we traversed the Cincinnati Bridge, across the Ohio River. As we entered Kentucky and the landscape began its gradual metamorphosis from riverbed to towering mountain peak, I fancied I could even see the Appalachians rearing their great heads in the distance. This milestone in our trip was the cue for Momma to reach for the cooler and prepare 'sammiches' for our consumption. Potty breaks were non-existent; hence, the coffee can.

After eating, Daddy reached for the eight track tape box and Momma just rolled her eyes, not big on music. It never crossed my mind that maybe she just wasn't big on Daddy's and my singing. Johnny Cash this time. As he crooned, *"Hey Porter, hey porter... how much longer will it be 'till we cross that Mason Dixon Line?"* Daddy and I would sing from the heart, sounding just like The Man in Black, at least in our own minds. Eventually, secure in the thought that soon I would see one of my favorite people, Uncle Tobe, I drifted off to sleep again.

Hours later, as the sun began the rapid phase of its westerly descent, we entered the foothills, then the mountains proper. Range after range, stretching as far as we could see—when we were high enough that we could see—colors gradually giving way to hazy blue until the mountains faded into the far distant horizon.

I could love these mountains; so serene, pastoral, calming to the soul. But by this point, I was tired of the whole ordeal: the pee-can, the bologna sandwiches again for supper, the noise of the old junker's unmuffled exhaust and the heavy odor of my parents' chain-smoking. Not even the thought of Uncle Tobe could cheer me up, and it would be hours yet before we would get to his house. Conversation and interest both lagging, I put my head back into my pillow to hide my nose from the smoke.

I couldn't understand Daddy's desire to go back to the mountains, and I certainly didn't understand why I had to be the one to always indulge his whims. Just because Momma was, by that point, usually in her own world because of a serious addiction to prescription drugs, why did that mean I had to get excited for a road trip that frequently ended in disaster? I suppose because Daddy was excited and in some weird way, looked to me for the support Momma was unable to give him. His excitement, of course, revolved in part around the home-made moonshine waiting for him when he got there. But I think the truth of the matter lay in the fact that Daddy was an Appalachian boy; his heart and his home was hidden in the mountains and rooted deeply in the culture. Only one generation removed, and I already could not understand my ancestry, but it did explain Daddy.

Suddenly the car lurched sharply around a hairpin curve, throwing me to one side and I sat bolt upright to hear my Momma scream, "Ken, slow down!"

My heart pounding like a trip-hammer, I thought it was ready to burst. Gritting his teeth, my Dad growled, "Shut up, Mae! I know these mountains like the back of my hand."

His clip-on sunglasses obscured his eyes, worn because the oncoming headlights hurt his eyes, even though no cars were anywhere in sight and the moon was just a pale orb, visible only now and again through the heavy dark clouds.

No longer sleepy, we all rode in grim silence as the darkness gradually gave way to a gray dawn, seemingly darker than the pale moonlit skies of the night just past. We entered the nowhere stretch, the longest part of the trip, blurs of the same trees for miles, just seen from different angles. Mom was back smoking. The food would be gone by the end of that ambient area. Heavy storm clouds, pregnant with the coming doom, closed in around us, around me, pressing down, down, slowly crushing the very life out of me. Despite the worsening conditions, my Dad navigated the highway as one possessed, straightaways and curves treated the same. Years of working in the coal mines and driving coal trucks on these gravel roads put the power in my Dad's hands to render Momma and I helpless, a state of terror which only fed his warped psyche. His sick laughter reminded me that we had traveled this path before, many times. My barely audible whimpers were drowned by the ranting curses emanating from the front seat. Screams of terror rose up inside me, threatening to overwhelm me, but I clamped my lips tightly shut; I did not dare let them be heard. I knew from past experience the more I screamed, the harder and faster Dad drove. I hated these mountains—so dark, so scary, tormenting.

The Appalachian Mountains are frightful—terrifyingly, dreadfully so.

Biology is the least of what makes someone a mother.

— OPRAH WINFREY —

SIXTEEN

"Rose is taking her trunk," Sue wailed.

My stomach knotted and flipped, and my mouth started to pucker and water. In seconds, I couldn't tell if the water in my eyes came from intense vomiting or tears.

"I'll see you every day," Rose promised as she caught a glimpse of my distress. She turned to put her trunk in the backseat.

I shook my head. Her words rang empty. I didn't want a promise of the future; I wanted her to take that trunk right back in the house and stay with me forever. But instead, she slammed the car door shut and drove off like she never wanted to look back.

As I watched her disappear down the driveway, an invisible clam-shell closed around me.

Looking back, the devastation I felt at that moment makes complete sense. Three moms in five years, then abandoned and without a mom at all. I am sure my Aunt Stella did not know that her personal plans to adopt me were not my parent's plans. I am equally certain that my biological mother did not know she was going to be bedridden with severe depression and, subsequently, a drug addiction that rendered her emotionally nonexistent. And though Rose never claimed the role of 'Mom' while she lived at home with us, it just naturally happened as she simply struggled to care for her siblings. When she left home, I suddenly found myself motherless.

And just as suddenly, adulthood happened to Rose: a husband, pregnant, a working dairy and crop farm, and the care of two aging in-laws. But she had promised; Sue and I spent as many evenings and weekends with our older sister as possible. Gradually, we started spending school nights and having the bus pick us up there, and then it was only a matter of time before everyone knew that Rose, at fifteen years old, had added to her job description by raising her two younger sisters.

I loved living with Rose and Butch, and all the experiences that that opportunity had to offer. Despite life's increasing challenges, caring for me and Sue was always of primary concern, and Rose's nurturing began to take effect in my life. My outlook and demeanor improved and I began to feel that I was simply in heaven. At Rose and Butch's, I knew the pleasure of a warm house, a bathtub, no loaded guns, the smell of fresh milk, the roar of a tractor starting, a full belly, falling asleep without the fear of tomorrow... Heaven, really.

Did I mention no loaded guns?

"MaryAnn, if you want to feed the calves, hop out of bed," Rose would say as she woke me. "The cows are crossing the street right now."

Instantly, I slipped out from under the covers and hurried to the window. I had the perfect view from my bedroom. I pulled back the curtains just in time to see the cows crossing from the pasture on the other side of the road toward the milking barn. I jumped up, hurried into my clothes and out the door. Just as the cows walked single file into the barn, headed for their milking stalls, I dashed in the door at the opposite end to see the calves.

Delighted to see so many adorable baby cows at once, I picked up the calf bottle from where I left it the night before and starting counting scoops of powdered formula into the bottle. Then I filled it with water, screwed the huge nipple in place, and shook it like crazy. The smell was so sweet and so comforting, both to me and to the calves, they all tried to nuzzle in to eat at the same time. I giggled, thrilled to be surrounded with their sweetness.

Since it was the weekend, I didn't have to hurry, and each calf got a full belly and lots of attention. The barn cats waited for me to leave so they could lap up all the milk that didn't quite make it to the calves' mouths; Momma cats and kittens—black, white, calico, tiger, gray—they all gathered to enjoy the goodness of farm life. I couldn't imagine a better way to spend a Saturday morning; no longer did newspapers with red X's line the floor.

Once all the calves were fed, I went into the big barn, where curiosity met wonder. The cows, heads locked into their individual stalls, mooed their hungry demands my way. I gave them each a huge scoop of great smelling food, which surely must have had honey as one of the ingredients. As the cows ate, Butch hooked up the milkers and, at the flip of a switch, I watched their udders sucked dry as the milk made its way down the glass pipes into the milk house where a five hundred gallon milk tank awaited its arrival. The process fascinated me.

Feeding and milking the cows took up a relatively short part of the day and, once they were let back out to pasture, the real work began, at least for the adults. For me, it was all fun and adventure, learning the art and science of farming out in the fields. And what fields!—acre after acre of corn, soybeans and hay. Beginning early in the spring, on weekends and after school, I helped in the fields—or, more accurately, rode the tractors as Butch drove the massive machines across the endless fields—plowing, planting and tilling the rich black soil of southeastern Michigan. The roar of the tractors gave me goose bumps; how I loved to feel power vibrating my body from tummy to toes as I perched on the wheel cover of the big John Deere. For the longest time, I was only allowed to ride beside Butch and observe, but he promised if I paid attention and learned to appreciate the power of the machines, I could someday be the driver. That idea thrilled me like few other things.

And so spring passed into summer as the corn grew from tiny

green shoots to stalks taller than Butch, complete with full ears of golden corn topped with silky tassels waving in the bright sunshine. Two and sometimes three times each summer, we cut and baled the hay fields to be put away for winter feeding of the cattle. Regular cultivation and fertilization produced bumper crops of corn and soybeans destined to be turned either into feed or profit.

As the weather turned cool and the trees began their metamorphosis into a monumental art gallery, field after field was picked clean, harvested crops stored or transported to the mill, as was their destiny. The sound of the corn as it was shucked off the cob and spit into the hopper became the music of my soul. Scooping handfuls of soybeans and letting them sift through my fingers soothed me like a good back rub. As the hay was baled, then loaded onto the conveyer belt to be stowed in the hayloft, it seemed I was watching presents being wrapped and put under the tree. So very happily, many seasons of planting and harvest came and went, and, as promised, I eventually earned the right to drive the tractor.

But above and beyond the joys of farm life, I also learned what it meant to be part of a loving family. Suddenly, I was a big sister. It felt right. I belonged. Each day strengthened the bonds with my 'new' parents, brothers and sister; and each day the shell surrounding my spirit and my emotions opened more and more.

Soon after my arrival, Rose and Butch provided me with eyeglasses. Eyeglasses! For the first time in my life, I could clearly see color and beauty. This combination of new glasses and new family opened a whole new world where everything was beautiful. So many wonderful experiences unfolded in those years, my spirit soared. I felt truly alive. I spent four wonderful, glorious years in the warmth of this love.

And then, as abruptly as my dream-life on the farm started, it ended.

Descending from the steps of the school bus and walking into the house, I saw my biological parents sitting at the table with Rose and Butch. The silence stabbed me, leaving behind its scars.

Brusquely Mom said, "We have all your stuff packed. Come on, let's go home."

As my stomach plummeted to the floor, I looked at Rose, and she matched my sadness, tear for tear. Rose was my Mom, and then she wasn't, and then she was, and then she wasn't again. Just like that. I didn't have a choice.

And just like that, the shell slammed shut.

It was real. Aching in every part of my body, I wanted nothing more at that moment than to be dead. "Please God, don't let this happen," I whispered, feeling as though no prayer ever mattered more.

"But what about the kids? I can't, I'm *not* leaving them. Never."

Jimmy, Amy and Jon, my younger 'siblings', along with my new Mom and Dad, had taken root in my heart and soul forever, for a lifetime. I could not allow this darkness of the night to steal away my family.

But the woman, who just the day before had dropped off a souvenir from her trip to the Appalachians like I was the little neighbor girl, repeated impatiently, "Come on! I said, let's go home."

"Dear God, I beg you, please don't let this happen."

But God had nothing to say that day.

The sun will not rise or set
without my notice, and thanks.

— WINSLOW HOMER —

SEVENTEEN

"Mom? Dad?" I whispered, the words more a prayer than plea. God might answer, but my parents would not.

I lay in the living room alone, the pain in my stomach intensifying in waves, each crest forcing me to bite my lip and squeeze my eyes shut against the tears. I cried and stared at the pitcher of ice water on the floor next to my pain pills, just out of reach, and told myself that they'd seen to me before leaving, that they cared enough to make sure I had my medicine and the means to swallow it down.

Pulling my thin blanket up to my chin, I flipped and flopped on the couch, desperate for relief. Sudden thrusts of pain split me in half, like a butcher knife stabbing me from inside out. I ground my teeth and clenched my pillow, determined not to scream, and battled the agony for what seemed like hours.

Exhausted, I called out to my parents in the next room, in the bed they never seemed to leave. No answer. I knew they wouldn't do anything to help me—it wasn't their way. Lord knew they'd already put themselves out by driving me home from the hospital that morning, another of the tasks they would have left to Rose, even though I lived with them, if she hadn't been away on vacation.

I tried to feel grateful that they had actually come to fetch me instead of giving the usual answer, "It'll just have to wait until Rose gets back; there's nothing we can do." Dad even drove carefully, for Dad, anyway; staying somewhere close to the speed limit and slowing down, instead of speeding up, for the turns. If he hadn't, I might just have lost my mind somewhere on the back roads between town and our house. My lifelong love of cars turned to terror in the days after the car accident that left me hospitalized for weeks and, for once, my Dad didn't use my fear against me.

I took a deep breath, my whole body throbbing, "Mom? Dad?" I called out again.

And again, they didn't answer. I knew they heard me; we couldn't help but hear one another in our house. I called out again and again, finally deciding that I would simply lie there and die while waiting for Rose to come home. Devastation filled me, and I almost gave up. What could I do? Having my Mama Rose living just down the road was always very difficult, and rather awkward, but right now it felt like a life or death situation; I needed my real Mom, Rose.

Like an angel, a comforting face floated across my mind and made me breathe a little easier. Just a few curves down the road from our house, Ruth was someone I'd sensed I could count on from a very young age. With her loving and caring personality, she was always very kind and oh-so-nice. She always wanted to help others, and seemed particularly drawn to me—poor, snotty nosed me. More than anything, I loved her smell—clean, fresh and powdery—a smell I innately knew I could trust.

Soft-spoken, a quality simply unheard of in my small sphere of people, Ruth's beautiful, soothing voice sounded both angelic and glamorous. She sang a lot, and to hear her calmed my soul. When I sat by her, she always wrapped her arms around me and let me cuddle in like a kitten. She felt so good; the warmth of her body and heart warmed me from the inside out.

Each day, as I knew my school bus neared Ruth's house, I leaned into my window, hoping to get a glimpse of her. Just that brief vision always brought a smile to my face. Sometimes, she would see me too, and wave like she'd spotted a long-lost friend. "Hey, Miss MaryAnn," she'd call, like I was someone important. Those days, nothing could get me down. Always, as the bus drove on past her house, I stretched my neck back to watch until every last bit of her disappeared, holding on to the sight and letting my shoulders relax as long as I could.

Suddenly, I knew what I had to do. I steeled myself before lifting my head and yelling as loud as I could manage. "Mom? Dad?'

Still no answer.

"I'm going to call Ruth."

Nothing.

It took a few tries to sit up and, each time, my head swam and my stomach lurched as I blacked out from the pain. More determined each time I awoke, I kept trying, concentrating just to dial Ruth's number. When I heard her voice on the other end of the phone, warmth seeped into my body and I burst into sobs. Weeping, I managed to tell her I was having the worst pain of my life.

"You stay right there, child," she said and, before I knew it, Ruth and I sat in the backseat as her husband drove us down my long driveway.

Her arms snuggled securely around me, I melted into the softness of her body as she began to sing. For the next 45 minutes, I drifted in and out of consciousness, but each time I woke up, I felt her warmth and heard her voice.

Either I'm alive in heaven, or I have passed on, but either way, this is like heaven. It even smells like heaven.

Back in the emergency room, the very last place I ever wanted to be again, my body pulsed with pain. I heard the doctors say they had to call my parents for permission to do emergency surgery, and then I was wheeled away. "Count backward for me," they instructed. "10, 9, 8, 7, 6..."

Coming to in the cold, sterile hospital room, my heart sank. There I was again; I'd only managed hours of freedom after four weeks of imprisonment. Then nurse told me, "We almost lost you again. Your body could not have handled the internal bleeding much longer."

My chest warmed at her words, instantly understanding that I'd been watched over far more than I knew.

I glanced around me. The angel Ruth was nowhere in sight. I knew she had been with me as I slept. The room smelled of her trustworthiness...

...or was it the newly placed planter of fresh African violets bearing the florist tag signed 'Tom Opal'?

If you live to be a hundred, I want to live to be

a hundred minus one day, so I never

have to live without you.

— WINNIE THE POOH —

EIGHTEEN

The sun, scorching hot and shining brightly, promised my favorite kind of day. The blue sky gleamed with the perfect amount of white fluffy clouds, each lined with silver, beautifully accenting the freshly manicured lawn that had either been blessed with just the right amount of rain or precisely watered by someone who took great pride in their work. As I looked at each family, stretching out a blanket to mark their spot at the annual church picnic at Frye Lake Campground, the image reminded me of a quilt, and the colorful warmth made me smile. Each blanket had a story in this church family, sewn together in patchwork squares; new, old, modern, traditional, ragged, colorful; each connected to the other, either directly or indirectly.

In the middle of all the blankets, the game coordinator held court, rounding up players for the next game; Donut-on-a-String. Rallying excitement as he wove in and out of the squares, a parade of people followed behind as he approached an area outlined with white chalk, designated for games and relays. Amused, I watched his entourage grow for the next game. Unable to help myself, I dashed forward, concentrating as the coordinator explained the rules.

The rules were simple: pick a partner, then one was to lie back on the ground while the other was to feed them a donut dangling from a long string. The first couple to successfully eat the freely swinging donut was the winner. Oh yeah, the donut was dipped in chocolate syrup, adding to the general hilarity of the game.

Twenty-one participants does not generally work for a game

requiring partners. Relatively unknown in this church, I quickly found myself the only one without a partner. Not to let anyone off the hook and determined to maintain the high level of whooping and hollering, the game coordinator made a play to even things out. "We need one more person," he yelled through his megaphone, voice as rich as a circus ringmaster.

Suddenly aware that all eyes were on me, standing alone, I inched back toward my family's colorful tapestry square. "That's ok. I'll just watch," I mumbled, trying desperately not to blush.

Rose, who long ago adopted the philosophy popularized in a Lee Ann Womack song—"If you get the chance to sit it out or dance... DANCE"—was not about to let me sit this one out. She quickly looked around, and spotted one young man still sitting on his blanket.

"Hey, will you be MaryAnn's partner?" she called out.

"I can't. I just had surgery," he answered.

Throwing her hands in the air, Rose grinned. "Well, all you have to do is lay on the ground. What's so hard about that?"

Peering past her, he said, "Who is MaryAnn?"

She pointed to me, and I tried not to let my buckling knees take me to the ground.

Our eyes locked and, with a little shrug as if to say, "Yeah, okay," he stood. Before I knew it, he was walking straight toward me, smiling what I would soon name the Tom Opal smile, a smile that could light up any room or situation faster than a match could set off a firecracker.

The clouds stood still as he moved closer. I held my breath, then gasped for air, suddenly worried I might pass out. Really? Tom Opal? This couldn't be real. Tall. Dark. Handsome. Perfect smile. Kind. Gentle. Intelligent. Funny. Articulate. Steady. Smooth. Really? My head buzzed. The air felt thin. Giddiness pushed sense out of my head. Tom Opal wants to marry me? Omigosh! How perfect!

I giggled as my thoughts soared and the seconds ticked, aware I danced with fantasy and not caring one bit. This was already the best church picnic I had ever been to and we'd only just arrived.

Thank you for being my partner, I would say with a supermodel's toss of my platinum locks. Thank you for waiting for me—the pleasure is all mine, he would reply and kiss my hand like a chivalrous knight.

Instead, unaware of my fantasies and completely ignorant of the fact that he wanted to marry me, Tom good-naturedly followed the game coordinator's instructions. Lying back on the soft grass, he squirmed to get comfortable while I stood over him—donut-on-a-string in my right hand, a bowl of chocolate syrup in my left, and my heart in my throat.

The megaphone squawked, "You must completely immerse the donut in the chocolate syrup, then feed it to your partner on the ground. The first one to finish the donut is the winner. On your mark, get set, go..."

Confident of our destiny, I quickly dipped the donut in the chocolate and lowered it toward Tom's mouth. The only problem was that my hands were shaking so badly—don't judge me; this was Tom Opal, you would be shaking too—that I absolutely could not get the donut to his mouth.

His forehead. Yes.

His eyes. Yes.

His chin, his ears. Yes and yes.

But not his mouth.

By now, the winner had been announced and Tom had yet to take even a single bite. The donut danced on the end of the string, jitterbugging to and fro, smearing chocolate syrup all over his face as the church crowd hooted and howled encouragement. Shaking with laughter, Tom finally gave up trying to even take a bite. I was laughing too, but out of nervousness and embarrassment. Everyone thought I was intentionally smearing the chocolate syrup. Absolutely not.

In fact, all I really wanted to do was impress Tom, or at least make him remember my name. This was serious business, of the greatest importance, but apparently, neither my hands nor the rest my body received that memo. Momentarily mortified, I learned that not being in complete control sometimes works out for the best. Though I didn't win the game, I won the day.

Tom has never forgotten my name.

Lots of people want to ride with you in the limo,
but what you want is someone who will take the
bus with you when the limo breaks down.

— OPRAH WINFREY —

NINETEEN

Happy birthday to you. Happy birthday to you. Happy birthday, dear MaryAnn, happy birthday to you.

"What did you wish for?" asked my friends, almost in unison.

I sighed behind my huge smile. There were so many things I could wish for, but I had already used my three wishes, and I knew God paid attention to such things, so I didn't make any wish at all. Instead, I stared at the happy faces all around me, at the gaggle of jumping, giggling girls, the likes of which had never been seen within the dingy walls of my home, and tried to keep from pinching myself.

My very first birthday party with friends. After begging and begging Mom and Dad not only for a party but for a *sleepover* party, and after listening to so many adult reasons why such a thing wasn't a good idea, I had won, and now I didn't quite know what to do with myself.

My friends rode home with me on the school bus and, as usual, Dad met me at the end of the drive to protect me from Rex. My friends laughed when I told them why he stood there with that big stick, that nervous sort of laughter that means you hope what you're hearing really isn't the truth, and then we all walked the long driveway together, each of them startling at every twig snap and frog croak.

When we made it to the house without seeing Rex I saw them all relax a little, and then watched their eyes slowly trace the sagging lines of our house as they stepped gingerly on the splintered stairs leading up to the porch. Our tiny aluminum kitchen table was covered with a plastic birthday tablecloth with balloons on it, matching the inflated balloons my Dad taped all around the kitchen. Displayed in the middle of the table was a birthday cake Mom baked just for me, surrounded by presents. I giggled. Now *this* was a real party.

Pulling the candles out of the cake, I realized there were just enough for everyone to lick the yummy frosting off the bottom—Mom, Dad, my three best friends, Jap, and the man who lived in the basement—yep, just the right amount of candles. I savored the taste of sugar on my tongue and tried to take a picture with my mind, so I could think about my birthday party later, when happy thoughts weren't so easy to come by. Smiling my biggest smile, I realized I felt normal, at least like I had always imagined a girl my age should feel on her birthday.

It was the best day of my life.

After the cake, I wanted to show my friends the best part of my world, so we headed outside. I showed them the pigs in the pigpen and the bench in the feeding coop where Mom and I sat if we had to hide from Dad, though I kept that last part to myself. I showed them the chickens and how we gathered eggs. Staying a chain length away from our junkyard dog, I told them how Dad mixed gunpowder into the dog food to keep him mean and make him a better watchdog. The path worn in a circle around his doghouse, the thick chain around his neck and his furious bark made my friends even more afraid of him, and they edged back as far as they could.

I smiled and danced around in the tall grass, trying to think of where to go next. This was the first time any of them had ever been to my house. I had so much I wanted to show them.

"Why don't you mow your lawn?" Dawn asked.

I didn't think anything of the question until I turned to answer her and saw her face. Her wide eyes showed fear and my stomach dropped. I had been so busy sharing the great outdoors with my friends that I hadn't even noticed how pale her face had gotten. "The goats and the cow like to eat it, and besides, it makes a great place to play hide and seek," I laughed.

She gave me the strangest look, and we kept walking. I headed toward the tree house that my siblings and I built ourselves, feeling so proud. I led the way as we climbed up into the big tree and stepped into one of the greatest places ever. I loved that tree house.

As soon as we settled in, Dawn, looking more and more pale, said, "I need to call my Mom."

I felt myself frown but willed it away. We had just gotten in the tree house, and I had planned to stay awhile and share the experience of it with my friends. Instead, we began the downward descent to the ground. No one asked why Dawn needed to call her Mom. Somehow, we all knew.

As it neared dark on that Friday night, we all waited on the porch to wave goodbye to Dawn, then the other girls and I went inside. We walked in the back door, went through the kitchen and past my Mom and Dad's room, where they sat up in bed smoking. With only two more rooms in our house, we crossed the living room and went into my bedroom, where we played with the little doll Mom had made for me. Then we played checkers and rummy, my Dad's favorite two games, and he taught me I should always play to win.

"Where's your bathroom?" Connie asked.

"Oh come on, I'll take you," I said.

Like little girls tend to do, we all headed to the bathroom together, through the living room and through the kitchen, where I stopped to turn on the porch light before heading out the back door.

"Wait, I have to go to the bathroom before we go outside," Connie said.

As I turned to tell her that was where we were going, I froze. My face flushed in horror. In all my planning, I did not plan for this minute. Connie walked back through the kitchen, as if she'd forgotten she needed to go to the bathroom.

"I need to call my Mom," Sheila quavered.

No one asked why. Somehow, we all knew.

Though it seemed like a different world, Sheila only lived a paved road away from us, and her Mom and Dad were there in no time to pick her up. Before we went back inside, I asked Connie if she still needed to go to the bathroom, and she said yes. We turned and headed away from the house.

If one had to be introduced to an outhouse in Michigan, mid-April was the best time; not too hot, which makes the smell almost unbearable, and not too cold, which means exposing the body to cold where cold shouldn't be.

Though it was obviously her first experience using an outhouse, Connie didn't run, and actually seemed intrigued. I waited outside the little booth for her to finish, and when she emerged, her interest piqued and fulfilled without a mad dash to stifle, I knew she and I would be friends for life.

To change one's life: Start immediately.

Do it flamboyantly.

— WILLIAM JAMES —

TWENTY

It was the Summer of Love, and most of the world focused on drugs, sex, and rock n' roll. Those who wanted a debate spent hours discussing whether the 'peace sign' was good or evil or what effect Apollo 11 would have on future generations.

As a young girl, my focus was much simpler: all things tie-dyed, boys, and cars. The roar of a powerful engine sent me squealing. My daydreams, a favorite and necessary pastime, usually centered on cars. Grabbing an imaginary gearshift, I cycled through the gears with one hand, while firmly grasping the steering wheel in the other, taking in the smell of its rich leather. Gradually, I pushed the gas pedal to accelerate and listened closely so I knew when to shift into a higher gear. Even the fantasized sound of gears slipping from one to the next made my ears tingle. The sensation of all the little hairs vibrating my eardrum felt so real that I reached up and scratched my ears.

The action made my ears feel better, but one day it also told me that I wasn't dreaming. That day, the sound was full and deep with no popping or crackling, a production of pure power. And although this kind of car did not come down our narrow, gravel road, I still knew what I was hearing: a muscle car.

Since early morning, I'd been waiting for my favorite aunt to arrive. As soon as Dad hung up the phone, I started dancing because I knew what he was going to say. "That was Aunt Stella. They're coming for a visit."

As his announcement sank in, my heart sank the tiniest bit in spite of myself. I knew exactly what a visit meant. Clear the clutter. Clean the fridge. Sweep. Mop. Dust. Try to make our tiny, four-room box look like more than what it was.

"Hurry," Mom panicked as she scurried to the sink with an apron full of produce. "We're running out of time. They could be here any second."

If we only needed to tidy the house, there wouldn't have been such a rush, but a visit always meant time in the garden too. City folks expected fresh vegetables when they came to the country, and we never left them disappointed.

Finally finished, house at its best, I had perched on my knees atop the kitchen chair, staring out the open window, and passed the time thinking about cars. And now, ears tingling and heart racing, I waited for the muscle car to come closer, tires rolling slowly on the gravel, achingly slow. Within minutes that seemed like hours, the car pulled into view.

My breath caught in my throat. A shiny, candy-apple red Mustang convertible pulled into our drive. Delight rolled through me, wiping away every trace of annoyance from the long, hot hours of cleaning and gardening. I no longer cared that I'd been sweating and uncomfortable just moments before. All I knew was how much I loved my aunt and uncle. An involuntary squeal emitted from my throat.

As the car came to a stop, I dashed out the back door to greet them. Hugs and kisses passed between us, followed by more hugs and kisses. Joy filled the sun-speckled air.

"Where did this come from, Aunt Stella?" I asked, unable to stop staring. I had never before seen such a beautiful car, made even more stunning with my aunt and uncle inside.

Aunt Stella smiled. "I just got it for my fortieth birthday. We thought a drive to the country would be the perfect place to try it out." She waved me closer. "You need to experience the feeling; there's nothing like it."

Before I was even conscious of moving, the luxurious leather upholstery caressed my skin. With only a shout to my parents, I settled myself into the seat and we took off down the driveway. I had to pinch myself; only moments ago this was but a dream.

Top down, the wind filled my hair, flicking the ends every which way. The brilliant sun in my eyes had never felt so bright. Scenery flew by, a Monet rush of trees and grass in green. So natural and perfect, the feeling was indescribable; so good and free. Pure delight, and, it seemed, objectless love.

I giggled with pleasure. The country roads around my home turned into magical pathways, beauty and adventure at every turn. For decades to come, every time I glimpsed a red Mustang convertible, my tummy tickled in the same glorious way.

More than thirty years later, as I sleepily walked into the kitchen for a cup of coffee, my eyes widened involuntarily as my focus was ripped from the coffee pot and I could only stare out the window. My mouth dropped open and my hands abandoned their search for a coffee mug. For a moment, I thought my aunt and uncle had driven to the country to wish me a happy 40th birthday. Moving in a daze, like sleepwalking in a dream, I opened the door and walked down the steps. A single tear glistened, blinding me, before trickling down the side of my cheek as I walked up to the fresh-off-the-showroom, candy-apple red Mustang convertible with a hand-written sign in the window: "Happy 40th Birthday, dreams really do come true."

The need for change bulldozed a road
down the center of my mind.

— MAYA ANGELOU —

TWENTY-ONE

"Your Aunt Stella ruined you. You're too big for your britches," whined Mom as I asked her to put out her cigarette before entering my bedroom.

I thought the big, handwritten 'No Smoking Allowed In This Room' sign on the door was pretty obvious, but apparently not. With so little air circulation in our house, something I realized when I deep-cleaned for Christmas and needed to wipe thick yellow smoke off the inside of the cupboards and off the ceilings, I wanted to prevent as much gunk as possible from settling in my lungs, as well as making sure my school clothes didn't stink.

That phrase, 'too big for your britches', was becoming something of a mantra to my Mom. She threw it at me often, and it both tormented and challenged me. Because she was ill after my birth, I spent the first six weeks of my life with my Aunt Stella and Uncle Del. And since my Mom had given away two other babies prior to my birth, they expected to adopt me and bonded with me as if I would always be their little girl. Of course, I don't remember my early life with Aunt Stella, but apparently that experience embedded itself into who I was, and who I was to become. Though I wanted to fit in with my Mom and Dad, to be loved by them, I also knew there was more and I had to find it. It wasn't a choice, but rather a drive.

And all the things Aunt Stella managed to have in her own life—a bathroom inside the house, pretty-smelling soaps and soft towels, a shiny car that started every time you turned the key—sparked a fire in me, a need to feel safe and clean and comfortable, to be the best I could be instead of just existing. That fire warmed me every time Mom talked about my 'britches', and, rather than scaring me back into submission, it reminded me that nothing would change unless I made it happen.

"What did you want to talk to me about?" Mom asked.

"I don't want to be a part of the free lunch program at school anymore."

"What! That's the stupidest thing I ever heard of! Free lunch and you wanna turn it down? Well, starve then, cuz we don't have money to pay for lunch every day."

"Mom, I'm not going to starve," I said. "I have a plan."

Mom didn't care much about hearing my plan since she couldn't even comprehend the idea of rejecting something that was free, but I shared it with her anyway. Having formed an entrepreneurial spirit based on Jap's example, I set my plan in motion. I regularly babysat for Rose and Butch's kids; Jim, Amy and Jon. I decided to ask Rose if she would pay me with a bagged lunch Monday through Friday instead of cash. "What a strange request," she responded, but the answer was yes if I could figure out a way to get my lunch every day.

Fortunate to be blessed with the best bus driver in the county, a woman who rescued me more than once in situations like this, I now feel quite sure she was another angel placed in my path for times such as those. Every day, the school bus made two rounds. Jim, Amy and Jon rode the first round, and I rode the second round. The plan was simple, and worked: each morning, as Rose packed lunches for her kids, she packed one for me as well. Her kids took the brown bag lunch on the bus and gave it to the bus driver, who held it until the second round when I got on the bus. She bade me good morning and discretely handed me the bag. No hot lunch at school compared to the taste of the lunch I had earned.

I think my issues with Mom might have been less problematic if I had stopped with just the lunch, but once I set things in motion, I liked being on the road to change, a path my Mom despised. Regardless, it was not long before I approached her with my next big idea.

Knowing that she would be a little more relaxed if she smoked a cigarette while talking, I decided to tackle the next subject in her bedroom. I sat on the edge of her bed and nervously waited until I had her attention.

"I know we don't have money for fancy clothes, but I could take what I have and make them look so much nicer if I had an iron."

The only sound in the room was a chuckle from my Dad's side of the bed. Until that point, I thought he was sleeping.

"MaryAnn, I don't know where all this is comin' from, but it's gotta stop," she sputtered. "You're outgrowin' your raisings. I knew your Aunt Stella ruined you." With that, she put out her cigarette and sank down into the bed, pulling the covers snugly over her body.

"Dad?" I said. I knew I would not get a second chance with this conversation, so I pressed on. "An iron doesn't cost that much, and I'd be willing to... "

"MaryAnn, stop bothering your mother and me with this foolishness," he mumbled. With that, he rolled over and turned up WJR on the radio, so that Ernie Harwell, Voice of the Detroit Tigers, drowned out any further conversation. Daddy loved the Tigers.

I walked out of their bedroom knowing I was on my own. I didn't belong in that place or in that life. I was going to get out, because I simply could not stay.

The only love worthy of a name

is unconditional.

—JOHN POWELL—

TWENTY-TWO

Years and years of rolling and smoking Bugler cigarettes stained my mother's gnawed fingertips a dense, jaundiced yellow. Those fingers had a distinct smell, cigarettes and coffee, a scent that almost caused me to spill my tummy. Everyone adored her for her unfailing love and her infectious smile, and her hands were an instrument of her soul. Without fail, a box always stood ready in the corner of our living room for any animal needing to be nursed back to health. I took great pride in our little animal hospital, watching my mother's every movement and wondering how she seemed to know exactly what each little creature needed in order to get better. Not surprisingly, it was equally common for a wounded person to find shelter in our Michigan basement or our detached garage; Mom loved their insides and bandaged their outsides, which together brought healing to many animals and people.

But what doctor can cure herself? She suffered from depression, severe depression. She fought it for a long time, during which she was a great southern cook, an active gardener, and an adorer of the outdoors. I loved being around her; the light of her smile seemed to shine as brightly as the sun. I followed her everywhere, studied the way she put chicken to fry and grew tomatoes the size of softballs. But over time, the depression, intensified by life with my Dad and our horrible home environment, won the battle. Mom started spending more and more time in bed, finding relief through prescribed medication.

"MaryAnn, your mother is sleeping, help me with these pills," my

Dad would say.

He and I would dump the powdery medicine from about half the capsules and then fill them with sugar. The task made me feel better and worse at the same time, both a patriot and a traitor.

"What are you going to do with the real medicine, Dad," I asked with the innocence of my age.

In his casual, business-as-usual tone, he said, "Oh, I'll just put it in this bag for now. We'll find a way to get rid of it later."

But something in his voice told me there was more to this than helping my Mom be free of her addiction. Each time I joined in his efforts, the knot in my stomach grew bigger, and the tension in our house intensified. Unaware she was taking sugar pills half the time, my Mom's cry for relief increased right along with the trafficking.

One night, Mom got up to see the medicine and sugar debris spread out across the kitchen table. "MaryAnn, why do you hate me? Why would you do this to me? I need that medicine."

I stared at her, unable to speak. There was no use trying to explain, no use trying to tell her how trapped I felt between my two parents, how I didn't want that medication in anyone's hands, how powerless I felt to help either of them. Tears streamed down both of our faces.

As time went on, prescription drugs took charge of my Mom's life; she was no longer in control. I longed for and missed her so much, my yearning made so much worse by the fact that she was right there in my house... and yet she wasn't. Her every day centered around the status of her prescription and how close she was to running out, while the quest for the next pain injection consumed her nights.

Every evening, lying in the next room, I listened through the walls as my Mom called her doctor over and over, begging for authorization to go the local hospital for a pain shot. He always started out the night saying no, but about five calls later, usually around two o'clock in the morning, he gave in.

I cursed that man every single night, knowing that he would put her—us—through this cycle, allowing her hysteria to peak and then rewarding her obsessive efforts with the ultimate prize, something I would then have to help her collect in the wee hours of the morning.

Already exhausted, I climbed into the car for the trip to the hospital and tried to catch a little sleep on the way, knowing it would be my responsibility to drive my sleepy, drug-addled mother back home again. Though years away from having a driver's license, I handled the car like a pro and never once fell asleep at the wheel, even after weeks and months of nights with only a small window of sleep between hospital visits and the morning school bus.

Years later, I formulated how I imagined a conversation would go when I finally confronted that doctor, when I let him know the pain his spineless actions caused, when I allowed myself to curse him to his face. Though, since I waited until after his death, I believe I let him off far too easily.

"Hello, doctor. This is MaryAnn. My mother, Mrs. Collins, was one of your patients; I'm going to guess you remember her."

"Oh yes, she was one of my favorite patients."

"Liar."

Uncomfortable silence. Dr. Thortman clears his throat.

"Now that I'm grown and have experienced a lot of life, as well as have some personal friends who are medical doctors, I have to ask you a question," I continue.

"Certainly, go ahead."

"My mother called you in the wee hours of the night, every night. She told you she was in unbearable pain and had to have relief. She asked you to authorize a 'pain shot' at the local hospital. Do you remember those years of sleepless nights?"

"Yes, MaryAnn, I do."

"Why, Dr. Thortman, did you tell her every night that this was the

last injection you could authorize, and then, every night when she called begging for more, you always gave in to her request?"

More silence and throat-clearing "Your mother was very convincing, and persistent, saying that she could not go on living with the intensity of pain she had," he finally says. "She begged and begged, and if I said no and hung up the phone, she would call right back. If I didn't say yes, I was sure to receive yet another call."

"So you gave it to her so she would stop calling you? You had the power to say no, but not the backbone? That was neither professional nor ethical."

"I'm sorry, MaryAnn."

"Those few years were the most difficult years of my life. I lost my Mom though she was still alive. Morphine made all her decisions until the day she died." I pause and take a deep breath. "And speaking of her death, thanks for the huge bouquet of white carnations. They reminded me of you—weak and without character."

This time, the silence is mine. Even imagined conversations deserve a satisfying finish. "Dr. Thortman," I whisper, "when I saw your picture in the obituaries, I thought about sending the same flowers that you sent to my Mom's funeral, but instead, I chose to send...nothing."

Dr. Thortman's shots usually lasted until I got home from school. One awful day, my heart sunk when I saw Dad wasn't at the end of the driveway to meet me. I picked up the big stick and headed up the drive with a show of bravado, furtively looking over my shoulders to see where Rex might be hiding, waiting for the lunge. As I got closer to the house, I heard my Mom crying for medicine and my Dad yelling, "You're a drug addict, Mae."

I sighed. My Mom never equated herself to a drug addict, she saw herself only as a person in great pain who needed medicine. She was, of course, both. As I walked into the kitchen, I leaned in their bedroom to let them know I was home. My stomach knotted at the helplessness in both of their eyes, and I just walked on into my bedroom and closed the door. Crying and yelling filled the house for what seemed like hours, and then I heard knocking on my door.

"MaryAnn, your Dad says you have my medicine."

I broke out in a cold sweat. Just like back in the days when my Dad was drinking and my Mom pulled me onto her lap because she knew Dad wouldn't hurt me. I'd been dragged thoughtlessly, carelessly into the middle yet again. Dad could not take what my Mom dished out when she wanted her medicine, so he often took the cowardly route and hid it in my room.

"MaryAnn, do you have my medicine?"

"No," I yelled through the double locked door, about ready to tear my hair out. I desperately wanted my Mom back, there was nothing I wished more than for her to stop taking those drugs. Since the only thing Dad and I knew to do was to take her medicine and dispense it as prescribed, hell became the new word for home.

"MaryAnn, please give me my medicine. Why do you hate me? Why do you want me to be in pain?"

I heard the desperation in my mother's gut-wrenching cry. By now, her body lay contorted outside my bedroom door.

"Mom, please just wait two more hours," I sobbed. "Mom, I love you. I would never hurt you. Mom, please, please, plea..."

As I lay in the fetal position on my bed, my whole body shaking with sobs, the person outside my bedroom door—known for her love and her bright smirk—began chopping at my door with an axe. Fear rose up inside me, freezing everything it touched. I knew this wasn't my mother. My mother would never terrify her little girl with an axe. No, this tormented being now splintering my soul along with the flimsy wooden door, wielding a tool that tomorrow she would not even have the strength to lift, was purely a drug addict. My mother would only return, albeit however briefly, after yet another dose of medication.

I pictured my Dad, lying in bed and puffing on a cigarette, as he yelled, "Mae, don't hurt my baby."

The screaming and crying continued until she forced my bedroom door down with a final swing of the double-bitted axe. As it came crashing to the floor, my body trembled at the most terrifying, yet somehow the most pitiful sight I have ever seen. Looming tall, dripping sweat, mighty weapon poised above her head like a movie villain, stood my Mom with a curtain of long strawberry blonde hair strung across her face.

With a moan, she crumpled into a little heap on the floor and cried, "Dear God, don't let me hurt MaryAnn."

I ran over to her, cuddled her in my arms like a baby, and said, "Mom, I love you."

Together, we sobbed.

There was nothing else to do.

Let the one among you who is without

sin be the first to cast a stone.

— JESUS CHRIST —

TWENTY-THREE

The silence was deafening. I trembled as the pressure closed in, made the walls seem to pull closer.

Somebody, please, say something.

Instead, I heard the cocking of a gun. My skin erupted with chills. Mom, are you really just going to sit there and let this happen? The room went silent again, silent but for the throbbing of my heart.

Eyes glued to the floor, my mind buzzed with questions. Do I dare look at him? Does he have his crazy eyes? I had to know. I just had to know. Slowly, I raised my head and saw what I had grown to fear most. Of course he had his crazy eyes, because he also had a gun.

My body seemed to crumble, weakened by a wave of memories. I thought of my brother and sisters, now far away, never to return because of those eyes. Broken dishes, splintered doors, broken bones. Everyone dear to my heart gone but for my faithful Mom, who stayed behind and fought the battles with me until her pain, physical and emotional, drove her to her pills, there to drift into a gentler, peaceful world where hatred and guns and crazy eyes did not exist. Her world, but not mine.

I struggled for a deep breath and tried to remember the splendor that could hide in his gaze, beautiful as the crystal blue ocean. His sweet, buttery voice drifted back to me. "I prayed for a princess and then you were born." I almost smiled and then caught myself; there was no ocean for me today.

Arm extended, pistol cocked, his eyes stared me down. My throat locked. No air, no pulse. Nothing but me, once again staring into the barrel of a loaded gun.

Even Loretta Lynn was silent.

Frozen, I waited for hours that could have been no more than seconds. He scowled and gave me the once over and then, clearly finding me lacking in something, his glare deepened. His finger moved toward the trigger with studied precision, all in slow motion. I watched, muscles tensed for the attack, as the trigger moved toward the handle of the pistol.

My world exploded in a mighty flash of light and the concussive force of a thunderclap erupting in a confined space. I fell to the floor. My flesh burned in places I did not expect, then numbed and grew cold.

So this was how Death happened; consciousness leaking out slowly, hope and strength dripping from the gaping wound of my heart to pool on the floor before running across the cheap linoleum and down into cracks in the floorboards. Thoughts of my life since I had to leave Jim, Amy and Jon, since I moved back into Mom and Dad's house, since Mom's drug addiction swirled in my mind and I came to the chilling realization that I had been slowly dying all this time. With that realization, came another—I welcomed this bullet that had just ended my pain.

But...

"I Can't Be Dead," I thought, because I heard, through the ringing in my ears, the frantic voice of my Mom, momentarily back in my world, calling for Rose to come to my rescue.

A part of me died that day, possibly the same part that died years earlier in Jay.

The part that only the future misses.

And the day came when the risk to remain

tight in a bud was more painful than

the risk it took to blossom.

⟶ ANAÏS NIN ⟵

TWENTY-FOUR

With my right hand on the Holy Bible, the judge asked, "Do you, MaryAnn Collins, swear to tell the truth, the whole truth, and nothing but the truth, so help you God?"

"I do," squeaked out of my 15-year-old, shaking vocal cords.

For an entire day, amid an ocean of tears, and in a courtroom that could have come straight out of a movie scene, I told the court all the details of my life. For hours the attorneys examined and cross-examined me. I knew I was doing the unforgiveable by sharing family secrets that had been preserved for generations, and my cheeks blazed hotter with every admission.

"Have your parents ever been abusive to you or your siblings?"

"How did your father make his money?"

"How often did the family make moonshine runs?"

"What kind of things happened between you and the people who rented the garage apartment?"

"Is it true that you have slept with a loaded gun next to your bed for your entire life?"

"Has your father ever fired his gun at you?"

I answered, as simply and truthfully as I could. The questions did not come as any surprise—I had told my story to the authorities several times by that point. What did shock me was how much sharper the words felt on my tongue that day in the courtroom, how slowly my mouth shaped itself around the answers, how hard I had to concentrate just to keep my lips moving.

I pushed myself, desperate to be done, to be gone. Forever. With intense focus, I looked above my mother's sad, lost gaze, and tried not to hear her when she whispered, "I'm so sorry, baby."

Finally, my part ended, I crumpled into my chair as if the day's pressure had ground my bones into powder.

Then it was my parents' turn. They were very short on words. My mom was flying high on prescribed drugs, and my dad could not quite grasp what was happening or even why. The whole thing would have made more sense to him if he could have resolved it with a showdown in the driveway, a smoking pistol in his hand, but this system had him lost and confused.

The attorney's examination faded to background noise as I now stared at my parents. I watched as they answered with almost childlike simplicity the harsh, biting queries of the prosecution. Questioned about the shooting incident, my father's response jerked the proceedings sharply into focus, the only response I clearly remember to this day, "Sir, I'm sorry if you disagree with the way I discipline my children."

The cross-examination of my parents finally ended and the gut-wrenching day came to a close along with the prosecution's arguments. The sound of the judge's gavel echoes in the courtroom of my mind; I can still hear his voice as he intoned, "MaryAnn Collins, I now pronounce you a ward of the State of Michigan. Your parents no longer have any privileges or responsibilities where you are concerned."

Mom and Dad looked at each other in total shock; a bucket of ice water thrown from the judge's hands would have been more expected than his words. My dad stood, but not as tall as usual, and my mom slithered down his leg, releasing the kind of sounds that come from an animal in unnatural pain.

Dad spoke for both of them, with all the sincerity of their hearts, with as much love as any parents could have for their child, and with eyes as pitiful as a well-loved puppy left behind at the county pound.

"We did the best we could."

Sobbing uncontrollably, they were escorted out of the courtroom.

I watched them go, feeling more alone than free, more confused than right.

...and this is where my journey begins.

Dear God,

I still love being outdoors, seeing you in the clouds, and at night, seeing you in the stars. When I am outside, I feel you right next to me; sometimes I even feel you hugging me. Some things never change.

You, the God of the Universe, are so much bigger than the God of my Sunday School, and so much simpler; "Love God. Love Others."

I love talking to you, and I try not to ask for too much. Today I am fifty years old and have been thinking all day of the things I asked of you as a five-year-old. I asked you a big favor, and as promised I did my part and worked really, really hard. I did not leave all the work up to you.

You were pretty amazing in hearing my dreams: I have matching furniture, I married an absolutely wonderful man, and though I don't speak perfectly, I think writing a book is pretty dang good for a girl raised on Appalachian-ese.

Oh, and I hope you don't mind that I shared our conversation. As I finished writing this book I realized, actually, it is a tribute to you, a whole life of you hearing and answering. The secret is out.

EPILOGUE

By Cindy Glenn
Talented Poet, Writer and Friend

The past,
Its weight nearly killed me,
trampled, then scattered me,
I was clearly undone.
Like the busted dishes lying,
on the dirty kitchen floor.

Hidden in the tall grass, I prayed to be away,
far away from the family that made their claim upon me.
Farther than that old outhouse that silently stood,
twenty feet apart from that windowless,
and unhappy, broken down house.

Gone from the man who held crazy like a trophy,
a bottle in the other.
Away from his bible that was ever present,
dwelling in the untamed turbulence, of his unforgiving heart.

Gone, from the woman who wore silence,
like a hard earned medal.
Blue eyes blinded by bright suffering,
shafts of love's white light,
and colorful confusion.

I ran from the mountains,
and retreated from the pain.
Like a dog licking its wound,
miraculously, I became whole and healed within.

It was the crazy that made me,
sane once again.
It was the wrongs, that made clear,
the path to right again.
The toxic faith which led me,
closer to him again.

The pain that strengthened me, I pulled deep from my flesh.
I Can't Be Dead, was far more than a flash of deep thought.

It's that which was heavy and weighted by hate,
That lightened and bloomed,
a metamorphism of sorts,
bestowed upon me, this beautiful gift.

Time stopped when I stared in the dead eye of that pistol,
A Smith and Wesson revelation, both ironic and painfully, simple.

My past, it's what saved me
And now the secret is out.

MANY THANKS

To Amy Rene, my greatest cheerleader while I was writing this book. Thank you, Amy for your daily encouragement, and for believing in me even when I forgot to believe in myself.

ENJOY THE RIDE
Words & Music By Amy R. Timbers
Dedicated to MaryAnn Opal

You've been in the driver's seat...all your life
Control in hand and in demand...
driving yourself mad—yah mad
What's all about? Do you think you have it all figured out?

 Why don't you take the back seat, and kick up your feet,
 Enjoy the ride, enjoy the ride
 Why don't you take the back seat, and kick up your feet,
 Enjoy the ride, enjoy the ride...Enjoy The Ride

You don't trust anyone...hey, that's okay
Calling shots and casting lots...
no love to give and none to get—none to get!
Always running away...you're never planning to stay

 Why don't you take the back seat, and kick up your feet,
 Enjoy the ride, enjoy the ride
 Why don't you take the back seat, and kick up your feet,
 Enjoy the ride, enjoy the ride...Enjoy The Ride

People and places...running through your mind
Was it real, hey-hey what's the deal?
So many wounds still bleedin'—yah bleedin.
Unable to give your best. So desperate for rest

    Why don't you take the back seat, and kick up your feet,
    Enjoy the ride, enjoy the ride
    Why don't you take the back seat, and kick up your feet,
    Enjoy the ride, enjoy the ride...Enjoy The Ride

Riding with Danger—she's your friend
Riding on empty—oh when's it gonna end
Running from devils, no one understands
Unacknowledged angels, oh, together hand in hand

    Why don't you take the back seat, and kick up your feet,
    Enjoy the ride, enjoy the ride
    Why don't you take the back seat, and kick up your feet,
    Enjoy the ride, enjoy the ride...Enjoy The Ride

MANY THANKS

To Richard Opal, my father-in-law, whom I miss tremendously.

There are many, many things I would like to say to you, but how to say them, and how detailed to get is another issue. I don't want this to end up a book. However, for the record, I'd like you to know that someday (and that's not a maybe) I will be writing a book and you'll be featured it. Why? The same reason I am writing you this note, because you have significantly impacted my life.

When I met the Opal Family, I was just a child—literally. Coming from the life I came from I thought you were all pretty strange. (Sometimes I still think that!) Please forgive me as I reminisce. Enjoy it with me.

I first knew you as my Vacation Bible School teacher. Never in my wildest dreams did I think someday you would be my father-in-law! I do remember Jesus shining through—brightly. You treated me just like you treated all the other kids in the class, it didn't seem to matter to you that I rode in on the church bus. Dad, I thank you for that.

I don't recall how much time elapsed, but my next vivid memory is my family (the Timbers) sitting at your dining room table and Tom riding by the bay window on a horse (with Roslyn on the back!). My imagination still plays tricks on me because I recall the horse being white and Tom looking like Prince Charming. Tom says the horse was definitely not white. But he was/is my Prince Charming. Anyway, when we went home that afternoon I told Rose, "I am going to marry Tom Opal." It did not matter that he didn't even know my name.

More time and lots of events later, I came to your house for my first Sunday dinner. I was very, very nervous. There were so many things I did not know. The first of which showed up when it was time to set the table. I was asked to set the silverware. Do what? I had never set a formal or semi-formal table, or do anything other than lay a knife, fork and spoon on the plate. Very graciously (and without anyone knowing) you showed me the simple way—knife and spoon on the right, fork on the left. My throat began to relax and I could breathe again. Dad, I thank you for that.

The very next week I went to the library and checked out Emily Post's Book of Etiquette. *I read it through twice before taking it back to make sure I had it firmly in my mind. I dare say I know more "proper etiquette" than most people.*

Over the next few years I learned much about life. I learned to appreciate so many of the things I never knew. Funny thing is, I never missed them because I never knew I didn't know them. God is so good like that. So many times I was in awe as I listened to your family conversations. I often thought, it's no wonder Tom is so smart, his knowledge came from growing up around this table. Without even knowing it, you taught me a lot.

I know the dating years were rough on you. I was a little young, a little poor, a little undereducated, a little different background, a little of a lot of things. If my boys make any of the same choices Tom made, I will warn them of all the same things you warned Tom about. It was during those restless nights of yours that Jesus began to answer your prayers without you knowing it. Though at first you had preferred Tom make other choices, you showed me love and compassion just the same. Just like you did in Vacation Bible School! Your love for me made a lasting impression on my heart. Dad, I thank you for that.

After Tom and I were married and we starting spending more time with our own family and less time with our extended families, I realized you not only were very learned, but very wise. Then I appreciated you even more. It was during those years that my love and respect grew and grew, finally to the point of this letter.

I've cried many tears about releasing you to the Father. However, I take comfort in hearing Jesus say to you, "Well done, my good and faithful servant, enter into joy today—what you did for the least of these, you did for me."

I love you.

MANY MORE THANKS

To my birth Mom who taught me about unconditional love, both for people and animals. And who believed and lived the life of a peacemaker.

To my birth Dad who taught me creativity, resourcefulness, the art of storytelling, and a love for music.

To the Appalachian Mountains, their beauty, their people and their culture. Fifty years later, I answer their call with a road trip to see their beauty and hear their secrets.

To Rose who became my Mom the minute I came home from the hospital. For believing in me, and for sacrificing for me. Always.

To Butch who took in a snotty-nosed brat. For always (always!) being there for me. And for being a real Dad to me and a true grandpa to my boys.

To Sue for being a warrior in the battle with me. For the memories. For the present when we both laugh and cry simultaneously.

To Jim, Amy and Jon who made room for a big sister. For sharing your Mom and Dad, and for sharing your childhood, you are the true heroes.

To Kathy who was willing to meet her biological family. For having an impact on my life long before we met.

And to my Kickstarter backers who supported this project. For a tangible display of encouragement through your investment in my dream, I thank you.